Bonaparte's Italian Campaigns 1796-7 & 1800

Bonaparte's
Italian Campaigns
1796-7 & 1800

George Hooper

LEONAUR

Bonaparte's
Italian Campaigns
1796-7 & 1800
by George Hooper

First published under the title
The Italian Campaigns
of General Bonaparte
in 1796-7 and 1800

Leonaur is an imprint
of Oakpast Ltd

ISBN: 978-1-84677-932-9 (hardcover)
ISBN: 978-1-84677-931-2 (softcover)

http://www.leonaur.com

Publisher's Notes

In the interests of authenticity, the spellings, grammar and place names
used have been retained from the original editions.

The opinions of the authors represent a view of events in which he
was a participant related from his own perspective,
as such the text is relevant as an historical document.

The views expressed in this book are not necessarily
those of the publisher.

Contents

Note to the reader
Written at the time of the war for the Unification of Italy

The following *Narrative of Bonaparte's Italian Campaigns* has been written, not with the view of imparting instruction to soldiers, for whom great men have written great books on the subject, but to recall to the recollection of the general reader, now that Italy is again invaded by a Bonaparte, the principal incidents in the marvellous campaigns of the founder of a dynasty renewed in our day. The book is written, by a civilian, for civilians, who like himself are interested in watching the development of great political and military projects, and who may desire to compare the present with the past.

The Emperor Napoleon III. has styled the famous Army of Italy which conquered at Lodi, Arcola, Rivoli, Marengo, the "elder sister" of that army which he is leading through the same land. This little book is the history in little of that "elder sister."

It remains only to be added that the basis of the first part of the work is the "Correspondence" of Napoleon I., published by the order of his nephew and successor, read by the light of other important works descriptive of these campaigns. But to the "orders" in that correspondence the author is most indebted, because they have afforded a chain of authentic dates, and a record of opinions and facts of the most authentic kind.

In the Appendix the reader will find some documentary matter, which, it is hoped, will be illustrative and interesting.

PART 1

CONQUEST OF NORTH ITALY, 1796-7

CHAPTER 1

Invasion of Italy

Sixty-three years ago, General Bonaparte quitted Paris to take command of the army of Italy, and entered Nice on the 27th of March. He was in the prime of his youth, and had not yet completed his seven-and-twentieth year. Fortune had favoured him, and he had made the most of every opportunity she had thrown in his path. Victorious at Toulon, the vanquisher of the sections in the streets of Paris, for two years his ardent mind, animated by a devouring ambition and passion for fame, had meditated plans for wresting Italy from the Germans. Under weak and mediocre chiefs he had warred in Liguria and among the passes of the Maritime Alps; and had already given indications of a power to conceive daring stratagems, and to compensate for want of numbers by superior skill.

But the hands to execute what the head had designed were feeble, and the young Corsican officer was only irritated and inflamed by the spectacle of the waste of means in operations without result, conducted on a theatre where he saw that so much could be accomplished which would encircle his name with glory. All was now changed. He had the chief command. He entered Nice in March, 1796, to make his first experiment as the leader of an army. In his view of the situation of affairs, the fatal blow to be struck at Austria must be struck in Lombardy; and he joined his little army, resolute to strike it with no indecisive hand.

The prospect before him would have damped the ardour of any other general. He had under his orders an army of 42,000 men, of whom about 38,000 were in a state to bear the fatigues of war. They were the toil-inured remains of republican armies, which had been wasted in aimless warfare. Throughout the winter many of these fervid soldiers, occupying the passes, and perched on the summits of the Maritime Alps, had been utterly neglected by the French Directory. They were clad in rags; they walked with shoeless feet; they had no money; and still worse, they had little food. The state of the army of the Alps, when Bonaparte arrived to lead it, would have satisfied that member of the Convention who exclaimed, "With bread and iron one can march to China!"—only, it had more iron than bread.

Bonaparte, on entering Nice, addressed his soldiers in a style destined to become so famous, and well calculated to rouse the spirit of a race always easily-fired by promises of the spoil and the glory of victory.

"Soldiers!" he said, "you are naked and badly fed; the Government owes you much, but for you it can do nothing. Your patience, the courage you have shown in the midst of these rocks, are admirable; but they procure you no glory—reflect upon you no lustre. I will lead you into the most fertile plains in the world. Rich provinces, great cities shall be in your power; there you will find honour, glory, wealth. Soldiers of Italy, will you be wanting either in courage or constancy?"

Recognizing, like Frederick the Prussian, how essential is the part which the belly plays in the movements of armies, he instantly began to provide subsistence for his troops. His presence and the energy of his commands, his great address, infused a new spirit into all the departments connected with the administration of the army. Seconded by the Commissary Chauvet, and by contractors like Collot, enforcing his orders at all points, he gathered up money, munitions, clothing, provisions, forage for the cavalry, shoes for the soldiers of all arms, new muskets for those who required them, carriages, mules, fresh meat and salt meat, grain, biscuit, vegetables, brandy. He impressed upon his subordinates the necessity of informing him of their wants, kept a sharp eye, and sometimes laid a swift hand, upon rogues who were cheating the public, and, what was more important in his eyes, frustrating his views and obstructing his plans. He desired to be informed of the names of officers fit to be employed. Every order was described as "urgent," every demand as "indispensable."

Commissaries were directed to sign contracts instantly. Officers were directed to obtain what was required, even in the so-called neutral territory of Genoa, by force, if it could not be obtained by moral suasion. Exact and frequent reports, it was impressed upon the staff of the divisions, were essential. The whole army was reorganized, magazines and workshops were established; rapidity, assiduity, accuracy, were demanded and obtained. After ten days of strenuous exertion, Bonaparte wrote to the Directory on the 6th of April—

I have still great obstacles to surmount, but they are surmountable.

The signal for offensive operations was the transfer of the general with his headquarters from Nice to Albenga, where he arrived on the 5th of April. He had been in Italy nine days. Five days later, he began in earnest that pursuit of glory, which, after twenty years of brilliant warfare, was arrested, at once and for ever, upon the field of Waterloo.

The task before Bonaparte was to break through the barrier of the Alps which separate France from Piedmont. On the western side there were three principal roads. One leads over the little St. Bernard into the valley of the Dora Baltea, shut at its gorge by the fort of Bard. The second passes through St. Jean de Maurienne and over Mont Cénis to Susa. The third traverses Mont Genevre, and leads by Fenestrelles and Pigneroli to Turin.

There is a fourth passage practicable for wheeled carriages in fine weather across the Col d'Argentiere.

A small army, under Kellerman, was posted on the French side of this mountain line, and on the other side, Kellerman's army was held in check by a Piedmontese force, commanded by the Prince de Carignano, and supported by the fortresses which the kings of Sardinia had erected to close the rugged passes against the armies of France. The force under Bonaparte was at the foot of the Maritime Alps and on their summits from the Col di Tenda to Voltri. The two principal passes were the Col di Tenda, a steep and difficult defile, leading upwards from Nice to the fortress of Coni in the valley of the Stura, and thence onward to Turin.

The second pass started from Genoa, traversed the Apennines through the Bochetta, and led directly to Gavi, Novi, and Alessandria. Between these two great roads there were several mountain paths—one from Voltri, two from Savona, a fourth from Loano, a fifth, practicable for artillery, from Oneglia to Ceva. These were extremely difficult; but it was Bonaparte's maxim that where two men could plant their feet, there an army could pass, and on that bold maxim he acted.

At the foot of these defiles ran the coast road from Nice to Genoa. It was, in 1796, little more than a track made along the beach, often confined by the sea on one side and precipitous rocks oil the other, to such narrow limits that only one carriage could pass. Yet this difficult road, within cannon-shot of the British cruisers, formed the only line of communication with France. The main body of the French army was seated on the coast. Augereau was at Loano, Massena at Finale, Laharpe at Savona, with an advanced post in Voltri, about ten miles from Genoa. Macquard, with 3,000 men, guarded the Col di Tenda, which by Bonaparte's devices had been won from the Piedmontese in 1794.

Serurier occupied Ormea, in the valley whence spring the waters of the Tanaro: and thus while Macquard held the key of the Alpine portal that gave access to Coni, Serurier possessed that which pointed directly to Ceva. What was destined to be the most important point in the whole line, the crown of the gorge on the road from Savona to Sassello, the Monte Legino, was held by a detachment of Laharpe's division and secured by three redoubts.

Piedmont was then in alliance with Austria, and the armies of these two powers were united to defend the Alpine barrier. The combined force amounted to 60,000 men. The Austrians were under Beaulieu, a veteran of the Seven Years' War, verging upon eighty years, brave, but not circumspect, and too much accustomed to the old school of warfare to contend with a young man who had drawn his science, not from the schools of the day, but from the great and perennial sources—the campaigns of the masters of their art—Hannibal, Alexander, and Caesar, Turenne, Frederick, and Marlborough. The General of the Piedmontese was Colli, an officer of only average capacity. In posting their soldiers the Allied generals had followed the initiative of the French.

The Prince of Carignano had scattered 25,000 men in detachments among the mountains from Mont Blanc to the Col d'Argentiere. They guarded the western Alps, and were a counterpoise to a smaller force under Kellerman. Colli had his headquarters at Ceva, because the snow obstructed operations against Coni, on the side of the Col di Tenda; and because at Ceva he could keep watch upon Serurier, who from Ormea looked down the valley of the Tanaro. Small detachments connected him loosely with the Austrian centre, under Argenteau, which stood at Sassello, forty miles from Ceva, and a little to the north of Montelegino, where Laharpe's detachment lay in its redoubts. Beaulieu, the commander-in-chief, was with the extreme left, above the Bochetta, on the road from Alessandria to Genoa, twenty-five miles from Sassello. Anyone who glances at the map may see at once how extended was the allied position, and how temptingly open to an inroad upon its centre, which, if successful, would cut the army asunder.

That he might induce Beaulieu still further to weaken his

centre, Bonaparte had recourse to a stratagem extremely simple, yet perfectly effective. The territory of the republic of Genoa lay on the right of the French line. Theoretically it was neutral ground, but the English had violated the neutrality of the port, by capturing *La Modeste,* a French frigate, under its guns; and the French General, Scherer, by way of reprisals, and to keep up a close communication with a city whence they drew so large a portion of their supplies that the soldiers styled Genoa *la mère nourricière,* had occupied Voltri and other points within the Genoese frontier.

When Bonaparte's arrangements were complete, he demanded from the republic a passage for his troops through Genoa, and thence into Piedmont by the Bochetta Pass. Had they consented, he would have instantly carried his army over the Bochetta, and have fallen upon the Austrian left. But they fulfilled his wishes far better by refusing, and, as he anticipated, by giving Beaulieu information of the intended movement. The effect of this news on the mind of Beaulieu was immediate. He resolved to assume the offensive, and to drive the French beyond the Var. With the larger part of his force he moved down the Bochetta Pass, while at the same time he directed Argenteau to advance from Sassello and occupy Savona.

But in removing his operations to the shores of the gulf of Genoa, he gave up all communication with Argenteau; and thus, while Bonaparte was about to strike, with the bulk of his army, upon one point, the Austrians in two bodies went to work upon two different and entirely disconnected lines. If Beaulieu met with obstruction, he could receive no aid from Argenteau; and if Argenteau were defeated, Beaulieu was certain to remain in ignorance of the event until too late to repair the damage; while Colli, far on the right, was imposed upon by the weak columns under Macquard and Serurier.

Argenteau quitted Sassello on the 10th of April, and marched towards Montenotte, while Beaulieu was hastening down the Apennines to Genoa. On the 11th, Argenteau fell smartly on the French troops occupying the redoubts on Monte Legino, the key of the road to Savona. To hold these fast became a point of the last importance; for the division of Laharpe was still struggling upwards, and Massena and Augereau were threading their way by another road over the Apennines, which led into the rear of Argenteau's position. Cervoni, also, at Voltri, was stoutly defending himself against the whole of Beaulieu's corps, and only yielding the ground inch by inch.

The ultimate success of Bonaparte depended upon the steadfastness of Rampon in the redoubts of Monte Legino, and Cervoni in rear of Voltri. For a moment, the Austrians under Argenteau seemed successful. They carried two of the redoubts by assault, but they dashed in vain against the third. Its defenders, at the instigation of Colonel Rampon, who knew how much his countrymen of that day, and perhaps of this, are fired by the solemnity of a great oath, swore to bury themselves in the ruins of the work rather than yield it to the enemy. All that long spring day the Austrian columns fiercely contended for possession of a mound of earth; and all day long, with admirable tenacity, Rampon and his men kept them at bay. But that mound of earth was worth defending; it was, for the moment, the pivot upon which turned the chances of the campaign.

And during that day, while Cervoni, deprived of all support, was rivalling the constancy of Rampon, Laharpe was urging his division up the southern slope of the Apennines to the succour of the defenders of the redoubt. When the light of the morrow's dawn stole over the broken ridges around, the sentries of Argenteau's army saw Laharpe's division in position behind the redoubt At the same time, Massena and Augereau had climbed the hills above Savona, passing by Altare, and arriving on the reverse slope, had headed their columns by Cadibona and Quiliano, for the rear of the Austrian army.

As the day grew apace, the republicans debouched from unlooked-for directions, and Argenteau found himself assailed in front and rear by nearly the whole of Bonaparte's army; for Cervoni, after having obstructed Beaulieu, who had mistaken his handful for the leading columns of the French main body, had decamped in the night, and had joined his division. Thus assaulted at Montenotte, Argenteau could not resist; and, breaking away in disorder, his men fled towards Dego, where they tallied their scattered regiments.

But the young invader, so far brilliantly successful, was only on the threshold of his gigantic task. He had pierced, but not quite severed, through the centre. Argenteau was forced back to Dego; Beaulieu, deceived and bewildered, was wandering in search of his communications with the rest of his army.

"Everything assures us," wrote Napoleon to Massena, on the 12th, "that the work of today and that of tomorrow will tell in history."

Bonaparte, whose activity was as prodigious as his judgement was sound and swift, had followed up his first blow by others struck with equal decision and energy, and intended to widen the gap between the wings of the allied army. Provera, with a small Austrian force, was at Cossaria, near Milesimo. It was intended that he should keep up a communication between Colli and Argenteau. He found himself isolated from his chief, and on the 13th, leaving Laharpe to watch for Beaulieu, Bonaparte, taking with him Augereau and Massena, fell upon Provera and drove him and his grenadiers into the *château* of Cossaria.

It might now have seemed practicable to turn upon the Piedmontese, and defeat them before dealing again with the Austrians. Bonaparte did not so determine. Argenteau was at Dego. Beaulieu had heard of his defeat, and, thinking he had fallen back to Sassello, was marching to join him. But instead of doing so with the bulk of his force, Beaulieu persisted in his old courses, and moving upon Acqui himself, sent Wukassowich across the hills towards Sassello. Bonaparte, believing that his opponents would strive to gather to a head about Dego, determined to prevent them by assailing Argenteau again. He, therefore, left Augereau to besiege Provera, and front the Piedmontese; and, joining Laharpe to Massena, hastened to Dego, and, having a superiority of numbers, forced Argenteau, who stoutly resisted, back upon Acqui.

The same day, Provera, after a splendid defence, surrendered to Augereau. As a measure of precaution, Bonaparte, while, fighting at Dego, had posted a few men in some redoubts on his right rear. Wukassowich, coming through Sassello, in search of Argenteau, much to his surprise, found these soldiers in his path; but, being a brave fellow, he assailed them with impetuosity, stormed the redoubts, expelled the garrison, pursued them sharply towards Dego, and threw the whole army into confusion. The French right was surprised in the disorder of yesterday's victory; Wukassowich pressed on with a fiery tread; one division of the French army gave way before five Austrian battalions; and it required all the efforts of the reserve under Massena to rally the fugitives, and to check the enemy. The gallant Illyrian was at length overpowered by numbers, and forced to fly to Acqui.

Bonaparte had now the upper hand of his enemies. On the 15th he was in a position to carry out the second and more important part of his plan. His first object, that of cutting asunder the two armies, he had accomplished in four days of rapid warfare. His second object was to press the Piedmontese with impetuosity, and force them to make a separate peace; and he was encouraged by knowing that Spanish intrigues at the Court of Turin had already sapped the weak resolution of Victor Amadeus. Without giving his enemies time to think or act, he marched against them on the morning of the 15th.

Serurier had been apprised of the successes of the main body in the two combats at Dego, and had been instructed to hold himself ready to move at a moment's warning. The Sardinians were in position on Montezemolo, west of Milesimo. Bonaparte assailed the position in front and on both flanks; Augereau broke in upon their front; Joubert, supported by Laharpe, who was directed upon Salicetto, turned the left by Rocca Vignale; while Rusca occupied a position commanding the valley of the Bormida, and Serurier, whose turn had come at last, easily pushed before him the outposts of the enemy, and effected a junction, with the main body at Montezemolo.

The Sardinians were now forced to retire into the entrenched camp and citadel of Ceva, Bonaparte, keeping Laharpe in his right rear to watch Beaulieu, who lingered, at Acqui, directed the bulk of his forces against the Sardinian position. Serurier and Joubert fell on the right and front; Augereau moved down the Tanaro, and crossing the river, menaced the left of the Sardinians by Castellino. The effect of these operations was that Colli, fearing to be cut off, evacuated Ceva, and retired behind the Cursaglia river. Pressing smartly on, Bonaparte assailed him in position, but met with a reverse at St, Michel.

The position was too strong, and he, therefore, obtained by manoeuvring what he could not obtain by main strength, Colli, apprehensive of being anticipated at Mondovi, retreated on the night of the 20th April, falling back towards that town. Well placed for pursuit, and inured to rapid marches, the French van closed with him at Vico; and after a stubborn combat, threatened again in his rear, the Sardinian general hurried through Mondovi, and hardly halted until he had placed the Stura between himself and his foes.

Bonaparte had now not only driven the allies far asunder, but had, in substituting the road by Ormea to Oneglia for that of Altare to Savona, shortened his own line of communication with France; and his despatches show how careful he was to guard this road.

The army had shown its bravery, endurance, and obedience— three capital qualities; it disgraced itself by its conduct after the combat :

"The Commander-in-Chief," said Bonaparte, in a General Order, "sees with horror the frightful pillage committed by perverse men who reach their corps when fighting is over, to give themselves up to excesses dishonourable to the French name. The soldier without bread gives way to an excess of fury which makes one blush to bear the name of man, I am determined to make some terrible examples. I will restore order, or cease to command these brigands."

Bonaparte now moved to his right down the valley of the Tanaro, in order to force the Piedmontese to fight or retire from Fossano. Investing the fortress of Cherasco which covered their front, he sent Augereau towards Alba, a town on the Tanaro, about thirty miles from Turin, and thus again alarmed Colli for his line of retreat Before his vigorous and incessant efforts all gave way. Colli was driven from Fossano, and Cherasco, which might have stood a siege, yielded to a powerful demonstration. On the 26th of April, fifteen days after Bonaparte had won his first victory, he had established his headquarters in Cherasco, and the enemy were at the gate soliciting an armistice. The Court of Turin were already alarmed at the progress of the republicans, and in order to augment their terrors, Bonaparte organized a democratic movement at Alba, and issued the following proclamation to his army:—

Headquarters, Cherasco, 26th April, 1796.

Soldiers!—You have in fifteen days achieved six victories, taken twenty-one colours, fifty-five pieces of cannon, several fortresses, and conquered the richest portion of Piedmont. You have taken 15,000 prisoners, and killed or wounded more than 10,000 men.

Hitherto you had fought for sterile rocks made illustrious by your courage, but useless to your country. At this day you are through your services the equals of the armies of Holland and the Rhine. Destitute of everything, you have yourselves sufficed for everything. You have gained battles without cannons, passed rivers without bridges, accomplished forced marches without shoes, bivouacked without brandy, and often without bread. Republican phalanxes, the soldiers of liberty, were alone capable of enduring what you have endured. Thanks be to you for this, Soldiers! A grateful country will owe to you her prosperity; and if, as victors of Toulon, you presaged the immortal campaign of 1794, your present victories presage one still finer.

The two armies which lately attacked you with boldness

are flying dismayed before you. The perverse men who laughed at your wretchedness, and rejoiced in thought at the triumphs of your enemies, are confounded and trembling.

But, Soldiers! you have done nothing,—since there still remains for you to do. Neither Turin nor Milan is yours. The ashes of the victors of Tarquin are still trodden by the assassins of Basseville! You were destitute of everything at the beginning of the campaign; you are now abundantly provided. The magazines taken from your enemies are numerous. The siege and field artillery have arrived. Soldiers! France has a right to expect great things of you. Will you justify her expectation?

The greatest obstacles are surmounted, no doubt; but you have still battles to fight, towns to take, rivers to pass. Is there one among you whose courage, relaxes? Is there one who would prefer to return, to endure patiently on the summits of the Alps and Apennines the insults of that slavish soldiery? No; there are not such among the victors of Montenotte, Milesimo, of Dego, and Mondovi? All are burning to bear far forth the glory of the French people. All are bent on humiliating those arrogant kings who dared to entertain the thought of imposing chains upon us. All are bent on dictating a glorious peace, and one which shall indemnify our country for the immense sacrifices she has made. All wish to be able to say proudly, when they return to their villages '*I belonged to the conquering army of Italy!*'

Friends! I promise you this conquest; but there is a condition, which you must swear to fulfil;—it is to respect the populations you deliver, to put down the horrible pillagings committed by villains set on by our enemies. Without this you would not be the liberators of the people, you would be their scourges; you would not be an honour to the French people, it would disavow you. Your victories, your courage, your successes, the blood of our brothers fallen in battle,—all would be lost—all, even honour and glory.

As for me, and the generals who possess your confidence, we should blush to command an army without discipline, without restraint, knowing no law but force. But, invested with the national authority, strong through justice, and through law, I shall know how to impose on that small number of men without courage and without heart, respect for the laws of humanity and honour, which they trample under foot.

I will not suffer brigands to sully your laurels. I will cause the regulation which I have inserted in the Order of the Day, to be rigorously executed. Pillagers shall be shot without mercy; several have been so already. I have had occasion to remark with pleasure the eagerness with which the good soldiers of the army have taken part in the execution of the orders.

People of Italy! the French army comes to break your chains. The French people is the friend of every people. Approach her with confidence. Your property, your religion, and your usages shall be respected.

We make war as generous enemies; we have no quarrel but with the tyrants who enthral you.

Bonaparte.

This fiery manifesto, combined with the impetuosity which had driven the Piedmontese, day after day, across their fertile valleys and fertilizing streams, and the bold countenance which had kept Beaulieu irresolute at Acqui, while his ally was ruined, produced an astonishing effect at Turin, where the Spanish party had paved the road that led to submission. Bonaparte knew his own weakness. But "*surveillance et jactance*" was his maxim, and while he boasted enough in his proclamation, he took every military precaution to secure his position, connect himself with the division on the Col di Tenda, communicate with the army of the Alps by detachments to his left, and hold himself in readiness to march forward, or dictate terms to his foes.

In Cherasco, standing at the junction of the Stura with the Tanaro, he had a strong support; in its magazines he found large stores of provisions, and on its ramparts twenty-eight cannons. On the 27th April he dictated the conditions upon which he would agree to an armistice; and on the 28th those conditions were signed. The Piedmontese gave up the fortress of Coni, which secured the road over the Col di Tenda, the fortresses of Alessandria and Tortona, which covered his intended line of operations against Lombardy, all the artillery and munitions in these places, and they ceeded the whole of the territory conquered by the French, to wit, the country between the Stura and the Bormida, with the road from Asti to the latter river for a northern limit.

Bonaparte also obtained the right to send his couriers and *aides-de-camp* by Turin and Susa to Paris, a concession that shortened by one half the distance between him and his Government; and he obtained by the fourth article the right to pass the Po at Valenza, the meaning of which we shall soon see. These immense results were the fruits of sixteen days of the most rapid warfare that modern Europe had beheld.

CHAPTER 2

Passage of the Po

Already Bonaparte had meditated his great plan for the invasion of Lombardy. The very day on which the armistice was signed, he wrote to the Directory that on the morrow he should be on the heels of Beaulieu, and that in a month he should be on the mountains of the Tyrol. Bonaparte at once put his army in motion, sending Laharpe to Acqui, whence Beaulieu fell back across the Po, and Augereau to Nizza. Orders were issued on all sides; some providing for the occupation of the fortresses, others dictating measures to secure the communications, others calling for horses, provisions, clothing. He was already anxious to impose a heavy contribution on the "*oligarchs*" of Genoa, and to persuade the Directory to promise Lombardy to the King of Sardinia, providing he would join the French with 15,000 men.

At this time, April 29th, he estimated his own army at 28,000, his adversary's at 26,000, his own horsemen at 3,600, Beaulieu's at 4,000. His only professed apprehension was that the Austrians would be too strong in cavalry. The whole French army not doing garrison duty was now on the march for the Po. Bonaparte was at Cherasco on the 29th, at Alba on the 30th, at Acqui on the same day. He looked confidently forward to victory, and, while the "*brigandage*" of his troops made him shudder with horror, he coolly meditated how he should spoil the small princes of Italy. On the 1st of May, he wrote from Acqui to the citizen Faypoult, at Genoa,—a letter in which is this instructive passage:—

"Send me," said he, "a note on the Dukes of Parma, Piacenza, and Modena; the forces they have on foot, the
strong places they possess, in what consists the wealth of
their countries. Especially send a note of the pictures, statues, cabinets, and curiosities which are at Milan, Parma,
Piacenza, Modena, Bologna."

And, a few days later, he informed the Directory that it would
be useful if they would send him three or four well-known artists, to choose such works of art as it would be convenient to
take and forward to Paris.

On arriving at Bosco, on the 2nd of May, Bonaparte began
to develop his plan for the invasion of Lombardy. The fourth
article in the armistice of Cherasco now came into play. He had
therein stipulated for the right to pass the Po at Valenza, a town
lying between Casale and Alessandria; and the better to deceive
his enemy, and make him believe that his front would be assailed, Bonaparte, in his communications with the Piedmontese
officials, whom he plied with delicate flattery, openly stated his
intention of availing himself of the stipulated right.

With similar view he posted Serurier at Valenza, but he carried the rest of his army to Sale, Castelazzo, Tortona. Keeping his
great design a profound secret, even from his own generals, he
ordered each division to select a battalion of grenadiers and a
battalion of *carabineers*; he drew 1,500 horsemen from Kilmaine's
division of cavalry, and six guns from the artillery of the army.
These picked men were directed to assemble at Casteggio, under General Dallemagne, and there await further orders.

This order was given on the 3rd of May, and on the 4th it
was executed. As the *corps d'élite* was destined to make a forced
march, he caused new shoes and provisions for two days to be
distributed to them; and he gave Dallemagne the young and
brilliant Lannes to command the grenadiers. While these preparations were in progress, each general was instructed to seize
the boats on the rivers, to cut off all communication across the
Po, and to impose on the enemy by military displays at Sale and
on the side of Valenza. As the time for the decisive action drew

nigh, the bulk of the force was marched still further eastward, and the officers were kept on the alert by repeated reminders of their duty.

In the meantime Beaulieu remained, in a state of expectation and apathy, in the Lomellina, between the Ticino and the Sesia and Po. General Liptay, with a small force, was between the Lambro and the Po; and Colli, who had taken service under Austria, was at Buffalora; on the Ticino, with a smaller force, separated entirely from the main body.

Now came the moment when all the parts of the delicate machinery, prepared with so much care and forethought, were to be combined and put in motion, to turn the flank of the Austrians, and fasten on their communications. On the evening of the 6th of May, Bonaparte, taking the command of Dallemagne's chosen corps, gave them the order to march by Broni and Castel San Giovanni for Piacenza. Before he quitted Tortona, he sent orders for the march of his divisions, to forward stations on the Piacenza road, but still short of that town, in order that if he failed to cross the Po, he might be able to return to his old positions.

As he rode along the right bank of the Po, he swept up all the boats he could find; they were but few. At Castel San Giovanni he directed a small advanced guard to get possession of the syndic of Piacenza, that through him he might be master of the population. On the morning of the 7th of May, Bonaparte entered Piacenza. The enemy had ho suspicion of his design. On the opposite bank were a handful of Austrian horse; Beaulieu still looked towards his front The crisis had arrived. Bonaparte resolved to throw his little column on to the Lombard shore; and at the same instant to send messengers with urgent orders to Laharpe, Augereau, Massena, to make a forced march upon Piacenza, and to Serurier to decamp from Valenza, and reach Piacenza in three days.

There were few boats, but they sufficed. Before nightfall the famous *corps d'élite*, Lannes at their head, horse and foot, and the division of General Laharpe, had stepped on the left bank; and

Bonaparte, with evident exultation, recorded the fact in an order of the day, beginning with the once magic words, "*Vive la Republique!*" This is the famous passage of the Po, a military exploit equal in skill to Marlborough's passage of the *nec plus ultra* lines of Villars, and far more decisive in its results.

The danger was not over; neither had Bonaparte secured his object—the enemy's line of communication by Pizzighettone with Mantua. Awakened from his dream of security by the news of the passage of the Po, and the march of the whole French army to Piacenza, the venerable Beaulieu directed Liptay to hasten to Fombio, a village in front of Laharpe's division, and to entrench himself there, in order that he might cover the road to Mantua. Liptay arrived on the 8th, and was instantly attacked by Dallemagne and Lannes, driven with much difficulty out of his position, pursued as far as Codogno, expelled from that village, and forced across the Adda into Pizzighettone.

Beaulieu had moved upon Casal, and, hoping to sustain Liptay, he marched in the night upon Codogno. In the thick darkness he surprised the French outposts, drove in the advanced guard, and fell upon Laharpe's division as they were rubbing their eyes and seizing their arms. Laharpe was shot dead by his own men as he rode in from a reconnaissance in front; his division fell into disorder; and had Beaulieu persisted, he might have routed the French, and have joined Liptay. He did not do so; and Berthier and Dallemagne hastening forward, found that he had quitted Casal, and retired up the Adda towards Lodi, at which place he had a bridge, and was once more on the direct road to the Mincio. But at Lodi he drew up, because Colli, moving from Buffalora by Milan, had not yet crossed the Adda.

During these encounters, Bonaparte remained at Piacenza. His infantry, still deficient in shoes, arrived slowly; and when they arrived, boats being scarce, they slowly crossed the broad river. The last brigades did not reach the Lombard bank until the 16th of May. Bonaparte took the opportunity afforded by the delay to force an armistice upon the Duke of Parma. He was compelled to pay ten millions of *livres*, in plate or in cash, to furnish horses, munitions, provisions, and his choicest works of art.

"I shall send you," wrote Bonaparte to Carnot on the 9th of May, "twenty pictures by the first masters—by Correggio and Michel Angelo."

To the Directory he wrote on the same day, "I will send you as soon as possible the finest pictures by Correggio; among others a 'Saint Jerome,' which I am told is a masterpiece. I confess that this saint has chosen a bad time to arrive in Paris; I trust you will accord him the honours of the Museum!"

And, conscious of his own ignorance of art, he reiterates his demand for artists who can select the best among the rich stores he thought it right to plunder. The soldier was forbidden to pillage, on pain of death; the general reduced pillage to a system.

That in the captain's but a choleric word,
Which in the soldier is flat blasphemy.

Having done all his work at Piacenza, and finding the enemy had escaped him during the delay at that place, Bonaparte departed on the 9th, and joined his army at Casal-Pusterlengo early on the morning of the 10th of May. Beaulieu was now in full retreat. Liptay had placed a small garrison in Pizzighettone to defend the passage, and Bonaparte left a division to mask the fort and cover his communications. With the rest of the army, except Serurier's division, he marched up the Adda to seize the bridge of Lodi. Beaulieu had decamped from that place, leaving a rear guard in Lodi and twenty guns on the left bank of the Adda, with orders to maintain the bridge as long as possible.

Lodi is on the right bank of the Adda; the bridge, long and narrow, stretched across from the town to the opposite bank, and had several arches dry when the river was not swollen by floods. The rear guard, placed in Lodi to gather up a small column which had not rejoined the main body, was swiftly driven out of the town and across the bridge. Bonaparte, after a strife of artillery, formed that close column of grenadiers and *carab-*

ineers whose charge over the bridge of Lodi has become so famous. Protected for a time by the town, they were suddenly led forward into the hail of balls and grapeshot from twenty guns which poured along the narrow path.

In vain they strove to pass the line where the shot fell most thickly; they hesitated on their deadly path. Seeing them waver, and knowing how soon a panic follows a check, Berthier, Massena, Lannes, and others—but not Bonaparte, as is so often stated—rushed forward to lead them. Some soldiers, dropping over the bridge, waded through the shallows, formed a line of skirmishers, and strove to keep down the fire of the guns. Perseverance and enthusiasm, favoured by a want of foresight on the part of the Austrians, who had placed no guns to crush the head of the column as it emerged from the bridge, at length enabled the French to triumph.

The grenadiers, with noble resolution, passed the fatal defile at a run, dashed upon the artillery, and aided by their supports and some squadrons of horse which had forded the river, routed the enemy. They took some pieces, but the Austrians carried off the greater part of their artillery.

It was on this 10th of May that Bonaparte first felt, as he tells us, that he was destined to be great.

The battle of Lodi has been greatly magnified in the telling; but, allowing for exaggeration, the charge of the grenadiers remains a brilliant feat of arms. As usual, Bonaparte, in his despatches, has amplified every feature; yet he admits that the fatigues of marching and fighting prevented pursuit; and that the wreck of the beaten division joined Beaulieu at Crema, and retired through Cremona behind the Mincio. The most welcome result of the action of Lodi was the surrender of Pizzighettone, which not only removed an enemy, but gave the French general another and an important point of support in his long communications between the Adda and Nice.

Having secured Pizzighettone, and sent its little garrison forward on their way to the prisons of France, Bonaparte reconnoitred his whole front between Crema and the Po, and found no enemy. He then turned his attention to the security of his position. A garrison was placed in Pizzighettone. A grand guard of cavalry was quartered in Cremona. Small columns were thrown forward from Piacenza towards Parma, and along the southern bank of the Po, as far as Roncaglia. Lodi and its bridge-head were occupied, and troops were posted at Maleo and Codogno, in rear of Pizzighettone.

Chasseloup was ordered to prepare means for the siege of the castle of Milan, whither Massena was directed to march. Finally, Augereau was sent with a division composed of infantry and artillery alone to Pavia, where he was to seize and live upon the produce of requisitions. Always forecasting, Bonaparte directed that the corn and cattle extorted from Parma should be sent, the former to Tortona, the latter to Albenga for consumption during the winter. Before he quitted Lodi, Bonaparte informed the Directory in a triumphant strain that "the whole of Lombardy belonged to the Republic."

It was at this moment that the Directory had the folly to suggest that the army should be divided; that Kellerman should command one, and Bonaparte the other section, and that the operations should be distinct, one set directed against Rome, Tuscany and Naples, the other against the Austrians. They yielded to a remonstrance which their young officer had the boldness to forward by the next courier. All would be lost, he said, were Kellerman and he brought together. Kellerman would command as well as himself, but it would be better to have one bad general than two good ones. The Directory yielded to such unanswerable good sense, and Bonaparte's career was not suddenly cut short.

On the 16th of May Bonaparte followed his troops to Milan, and the same day he summoned Lieutenant Lamy, the governor of the castle, to capitulate. Lamy had no idea of giving way to a summons which he probably knew the French general could not enforce without bringing up his siege-train from Tortona; and, somewhat vexed, Bonaparte ordered up the heavy artillery. He remained a week in Milan, and did an immense amount of work. He took advantage of the short holiday which his troops enjoyed to complete their equipment as far as means would allow, for many were still in rags, deserving the title they had earned from their enemies, of *"les héros en guenilles"*

He sent out spies to Trente, Mantua, Trieste, to obtain correct intelligence "at any cost" He granted an armistice to the Duke of Modena, at an expense to this prince of 7,500,000 *livres*, provisions, powder, and munitions to the extent of 2,500,000 more; and he exacted twenty of his choicest works of art. At Milan also, he seized nine paintings, a cartoon, an antique vase, and four valuable manuscripts. He gave his troops one half their arrears. He forwarded to Paris six millions' worth of jewels, and silver bars, the produce of different contributions. He levied a contribution of twenty millions from the Milanese. He framed a government for them, and promised, but did not give them liberty. Every decree was to bear the words, "In the name of the French Republic."

And the very first decree of this kind was one to secure possession of the monuments of art and science in the conquered country, to provide for their transport to Paris, and to appoint one Tinet as "the agent with the army of Italy, charged to collect in the conquered country the pictures, *chefs-d'œuvre,* and other antique monuments judged worthy to be sent to Paris." The man who countersigned this decree bore the Italian name of Salicetti.

On the same day a proclamation was issued to the people of Lombardy, in which they were informed that the French Republic, which had sworn hatred to tyrants, had also sworn fraternity to every people; that the despot who had so long enslaved Lombardy, had caused great evils to France; that he had been driven out, and that as "the independence of Lombardy" depended on the success of the French, the people ought to second their efforts. Therefore, the people of Lombardy ought to feed their brothers, and pay 20,000,000—a poor reward, he said, to be offered by a country so fertile, if the people only would reflect on the advantage which ought to result from it to them.

This contribution was to be drawn from the rich, the easy classes, the priests; and if it were paid, then there should be payment, or at least promise of payment, for all further supplies. This was the mode in which Lombardy was gendered independent by the French. Bonaparte found in it more elements of revolution than in Piedmont, which he said was not at all ripe for revolution; and, as will be seen, he found some that he did not count upon.

On the 19th May he determined to send the army forward once more, and ordering the march of his divisions to the banks of the Adda, he issued the following address "To His Brothers in Arms"—one of the finest specimens of eloquent "*jactance*" to be found in history.

Headquarters, Milan, 20th May, 1796.

Soldiers!—You plunged like a torrent from the summit of the Apennines,—you overthrew, dispersed, scattered everything that opposed your march.

Piedmont, delivered from Austrian tyranny, gave itself up to its natural sentiments of peace and friendship for France.

Milan is yours; and the republican flag floats throughout all Lombardy.

The Dukes of Parma and Modena owe their political existence only to your generosity.

The army which menaced you with so much pride, no longer finds a barrier that can reassure it against your courage.

The Po, the Ticino, the Adda could not stop you a single day. These vaunted ramparts of Italy have been insufficient. You have surmounted them as rapidly as the Apennines.

All these successes have filled the heart of your country with joy. Your representatives have commanded a festival dedicated to your victories, to be celebrated in all the communes of the republic. There your fathers, your mothers, your wives, your sweethearts, rejoice in your success, and proudly boast of belonging to you.

Yes, Soldiers! you have done much; but does there then

remain no more for you to do? Shall it be said of us, that we knew how to conquer, but knew not how to profit by victory? Shall posterity reproach us with having found Capua in Lombardy? But I see you already rush to arms. You weary of a dastardly repose. The days lost for glory are lost for your happiness. Well, then, let us on. We have still forced marches to make; enemies to subdue; laurels to gather; insults to avenge.

Let those who have whetted the daggers of civil war in France,—who have basely assassinated our ministers, and burned our vessels at Toulon, tremble. The hour of vengeance has struck.

But let the people be free from uneasiness. We are friends of every people, and more particularly of the descendants of Brutus, of Scipio, and of the great men whom we have taken as models. To re-establish the Capitol,—to place there, with honour, the statues of the heroes who made themselves famous,—to awaken the Roman people, torpid through many ages of slavery: such will be the fruit of your victories. They will mark an epoch in after times. Yours will be the immortal glory of changing the face of the most beautiful part of Europe.

The French people, free and respected by the whole world, will give to Europe a glorious peace, which will indemnify it for the sacrifices of all kinds which it has made during the last six years. You will then return to your homes, and your fellow-citizens will say, as they point to you—'He belonged to the Army of Italy.'

Bonaparte.

Leaving Despinoy to carry on the siege of Milan, Bonaparte directed his divisions upon the Mincio: Kilmaine, with the horse, followed by Augereau and Massena, taking the road to Brescia, and Serurier moving cautiously on the right through Casal-Buttano, upon the Mella. Bonaparte quitted Milan on the 23rd of May. On the 24th he passed through Lodi to Crema. At Crema he heard that the Milanese was in revolt; but he did not arrest the forward movement of his soldiers. Sending off swift orders, to the troops at Lodi and Milan to deal instantly with the insurgents, he galloped on to Sonoino to assure himself of the safety of his front; and facing about, reached Milan on the same evening.

The next day he issued a proclamation to the people of Lombardy. He told them he pitied the poor people who had been misled into the last excesses against a republic and a brave army, which they misunderstood; and, faithful to the principles of the French nation, who warred not upon the people, he desired to leave open a door of repentance.

But those who, in twenty-four hours, shall not have laid down their arms, and sworn an oath of obedience to the Republic, shall be treated as rebels, and their villages shall be burned.

Despinoy had crushed the insurrection at Milan. Bonaparte hastened himself to Pavia, the seat of the revolt; and, storming the town, delivered it over to sack and pillage, and restored order. The people had spared the lives of his soldiers; he shot the popular chiefs, and declared that if the blood of one Frenchman had been shed he would have erected a tall column bearing the inscription—"Here stood the city of Pavia!"

At Milan, Despinoy was ordered to arrest and shoot all taken with arms in their hands, and to seize 200 hostages, and pack them off to Pavia and Tortona. Then hurrying back to his headquarters at Brescia, Bonaparte sent his divisions forward to beyond the Chiese, and then issued a fiery-proclamation to the people of the Milanese.

Telling them that they had been misled by the priests, nobles, and agents of Austria, he warned them that the French army would treat the peaceful inhabitants fraternally, but would be terrible as the fire from heaven to rebels, and the villages which protected them. Therefore, the general-in-chief declared all villages rebel who did not instantly lay down their arms, and directed them to be burned. All armed persons were to be shot.

All priests and nobles sent as hostages to France. Every village which sounded the tocsin should be burned. All districts where a Frenchman was assassinated were to give up the assassin, or pay a fine equal to a third of their annual contribution.

Every man found with a gun, to be shot out of hand. Every house wherein a gun was found, unless the proprietor named its owner, to be burned down. Every noble or rich man convicted of exciting the people, whether by dismissing his servants, or speaking against the French, was to be seized as a hostage.

"Be pitiless for revolted villages," wrote Bonaparte to Despinoy, "and execute my orders to the letter."

These swift and sanguinary measures, executed as ordered, for a time smothered the rage of the people against the army, and permitted its chief to continue his conquering career.

CHAPTER 3

Passage of the Mincio

Driven from the line of the Adda, the Austrian general crossed the Oglio, and took post behind the Mincio. The war had now been carried across the Venetian frontier—theoretically, neutral territory, but traversed at pleasure by both parties. Anxious to propitiate the French, the Venetians had, at their dictation, expelled the Bourbon Prince, afterwards Louis XVIII.; but they were not strong enough to defend the neutrality they had proclaimed. Beaulieu and Bonaparte, therefore, moved where they pleased in the States of Venice.

The country in which the hostile armies were about to operate is now one of the most remarkable military positions in the world. It was strong in 1796; it is far stronger now. On the north, the mountains of the Tyrol project, like a great bastion, into the fertile plains watered by the Adda, the Oglio, the Mincio, and the Adige—rivers that rise in the mountains, traverse their valleys, and, passing through the lakes of Northern Italy, creep lazily along the rich alluvial plain, and fall into the Po and the Adriatic. The lowlands between the Po and the Alps are nowhere more than fifty miles broad. The Po runs from west to east, its northern affluents from north to south; so that they intersect the plain, and form strong parallel lines of defence.

Beaulieu retired into the area between the Mincio and the Adige. Then, as now, the position of the Mincio was strengthened by the fort of Peschiera, situate on an island where the Mincio flows from the Lake of Garda, and the fortress of Mantua, also on an island, planted just where the Po and Mincio mingle their marshes. In like manner the line of the Adige was protected on the south by Legnago, then inconsiderable as a place of strength; and Verona on the north, covering the line of the Austrian retreat into the Tyrol. These forts formed a square, the northern face resting on the bulwark of the mountains, the southern covered by marshes.

Beaulieu, placing a strong garrison in Mantua, took up his position behind the Mincio; Liptay, the vanquished at Fombio, stood near Peschiera, with some 5,000 men; Beaulieu, with 8,000 men, occupied Valeggio as his centre, with a reserve, a little to the rear; Colli, with the left, 3,000 strong, was at Goito, where there was one bridge; and a smaller force was at Borghetto. In front of this line, on the right bank of the river, Beaulieu's horsemen patrolled, to keep watch on the advance of the French, and maintain the communication with Mantua. As the bridge of Borghetto was the weak point of the line, the detachment there was instructed to break the bridge, should it be assailed by a French column.

Now, this was precisely the point at which Bonaparte did intend to break through his enemy's line; And it will be seen how craftily and how swiftly he executed his project He did not return to his headquarters at Brescia until the 27th of May. At that time his main force was in rear of that town; the right held back. On the 20th, Kilmaine, with the cavalry, was ordered to Castiglione, on the highroad from Brescia to Goito. Augereau stood at Ponte San Marco, on the left; Massena, at Montechiaro; while Serurier, on the right, was brought further forward. Thus disposed, Bonaparte seemed intent upon surprising Peschiera, and interposing between the Austrians and the Tyrol. But the movements of his right, which was studiously kept a day's march in the rear, were concealed from his enemy, who thus wanted that correct information without which neither a good chief nor a numerous soldiery can prevail.

Late on the evening of the 29th, Bonaparte gave his final orders, and took care to inform his generals not only what each was directed to do, but to tell each what task had been allotted to his colleagues. His object was, by a sudden march from his centre, to seize the bridge of Borghetto, and break through the centre of the Austrian line.

Fortune favoured him, Beaulieu, who, until the very eve of the attack, had kept a reserve well in hand, now withdrew its battalions, and sent them to posts on the river which he feared were badly guarded. Bonaparte ordered Kilmaine with the advanced guard of grenadiers and horse to move at daybreak upon Borghetto; and with this leading column Bonaparte himself rode. Massena followed Kilmaine; Augereau, rallying the patrol on his left, approached Peschiera; and Serurier hastened up from the right, and occupied the attention of the Austrians about Goito.

No sooner had Kilmaine reached the outskirts of Borghetto, than he drove in the Austrian outposts; but these, reinforced from the left bank, assailed the French in turn. Their enemies were too numerous; they lost a gun, and retired over the bridge. It so happened that, in the hurry of their retreat, some were pitched over the bridge; and Gardanne, a tall and brave soldier, perceiving by this that the river was fordable, led his grenadiers into the water, while the French artillery sent a storm of balls above their heads, and protected the passage.

Then the centre column assailed the bridge, and the Austrians strove to destroy it. One arch was cut when the flank attack of Gardanne began to tell, and the enemy was driven from the bridge. A *carabineer* leaped over the chasm, and, by his aid, the bridge was sufficiently repaired, under fire, to admit of the column passing to the left bank. Dallemagne, joining Gardanne's daring sections, followed the retiring Austrians until stopped before an old castle, into which the enemy had thrown themselves; and the sturdy garrison so sharply repelled every attack, that the French had. once more to turn the post This was decisive; the garrison fled, the French pursued; both entered Valeggio together, and Beaulieu, who was there, had to ride fast to evade capture.

The reader will remember that Augereau had marched upon

the Mincio, below Peschiera, intending to cross the river, and seize Castelnuovo on the Austrian line of retreat At first Beaulieu was ignorant of this, and gathering up his centre, he held his ground for a time between Valeggio and Villafranca, gallantly charging the French, and compelling them to give ground. Bonaparte was most anxious to encourage him to stand firm, because he hoped that Augereau would cut him off at Castelnuovo, while Massena established on the left bank of the Mincio, at Borghetto, protected the French rear, and interposed between the Austrian centre and their left at Goito.

Bonaparte did not press forward, but plied the enemy with cannon. In the meantime, Augereau had also crossed the Mincio, and wheeling his column to the left, marched up the left bank towards Peschiera. Liptay had been ordered to quit that fort, and join his chief by Castelnuovo. Augereau came up just as Liptay was engaged in forming his column. The Austrian saw that safety lay in daring; and he, therefore, fell upon the Frenchman so fiercely, that the head of Augereau's column was rudely pushed back, and 200 men were killed, wounded, or drowned in the Mincio. This saved Liptay, and gave him time to retreat in safety.

Beaulieu, hearing of the flank movement of Augereau, at once comprehended the unaccountable inactivity of Bonaparte, which had been limited to a cannonade, and several charges of cavalry led by the young Murat, just then emerging from obscurity. Beaulieu, therefore, withdrew in good order while he had time, joined Liptay in the evening at Castelnuovo, and retreated in haste behind the line of the Adige.

The Austrian left, severed from the main body, were amused early in the morning by the demonstrations of Serurier. Learning the truth, they sought to recover their communications; and hastening up the Mincio, plunged suddenly upon the French outposts in rear of Valeggio, where Bonaparte had his headquarters. But, seeing that the French were strong, the Austrian general rallied his men, and, fighting with his rear-guard, made good his retreat by cross roads. Colli, who had been idle at Goito, was not so fortunate. He was compelled to divide his force; following the traces of Beaulieu with his cavalry, and sending his infantry into Mantua. The Austrian general had hurriedly traversed the Adige at Verona, and marching rapidly up the left bank, placed his handful of troops in momentary security at Roveredo and Caliano, a few miles south of Trent

Bonaparte was not a general to sleep upon a victory so decisive. The same night Augereau was ordered to seize Peschiera; he had already done so. Rusca was brought down from Salo, on the western bank of the Lake of Garda to the Mincio. Massena, Kilmaine, and Augereau, the latter leaving a garrison in Peschiera, were instructed to march upon Castelnuovo; and Serurier, ordered to be at Borghetto at one in the morning precisely, hastened to cross the Mincio.

These orders were executed on the 31st; and on the 1st of June Massena was in Verona, and the advanced posts of the republican army were on the spurs of the hills of Tyrol. Bonaparte had promised the Directory on the 28th of April, when he had just conquered an armistice from the Piedmontese, that before a month he hoped to be on the Tyrolese hills. Our narrative had shown how nearly he kept his word. He had fought and manoeuvred his way from Cherasco to the rugged heights of Monte Baldo above Verona in thirty-three days.

In addition to the grateful news of these successes, a sum of 2,000,000 in cash, and instructions to draw upon him for four or five millions, Bonaparte forwarded to the Directory on the 1st of June two hundred carriage-horses, the finest he could select in Lombardy. "They will replace," said he, "the poor hacks who now draw your carriages"—a piece of superb condescension which must have irritated as well as flattered his employers.

During the next thirty days, Bonaparte displayed immense activity. His first care was to move a strong force to blockade Mantua, and to press the siege of the Castle of Milan, which gave him much vexation. To effect the former, Augereau and Serurier marched rapidly down the Mincio. It is remarkable how slight an influence, so far, Mantua appeared to have on the campaign. Bonaparte followed the soundest of rules when, by operating upon the southern shore of the Garda Lake, he compelled Beaulieu to remove the bulk of his small army from the neighbourhood of Mantua, in order to secure his retreat. Beaulieu defeated, Mantua was isolated, and its garrison of 10,000 or 12,000 shut up in the place. The French General could now safely turn his attention first to the investment, and next to the siege of the place.

Before he quitted Peschiera, Bonaparte entrusted one half of his army to the command of Massena, who, from his headquarters at Verona, was enjoined to keep a strict watch upon the Austrians in the Tyrol. Rivoli was occupied on one side of the lake, and Salo on the other; the great camp being between Verona and Peschiera. Legnago was also garrisoned, and the engineer, Chasseloup, received instructions to make the most of its defences, as well as those of Verona and Peschiera. Verona was the key of the whole position. It had three bridges over the Adige; it could not be carried by a *coup-de-main;* it gave the French the opportunity of operating on either bank; it afforded quarters, magazines, and hospitals.

That it was part of the territory of Venice did not prevent the French from dealing with it as masters. Bonaparte bullied the officials of that feeble State, and only kept such measures with them as made them fear and respect him. In reporting his proceedings to the Directory, Bonaparte frankly said that he had expressly brought about the species of rupture existing, in order that he might, if the Directory desired it, extract some five or six millions from the Venetians. His pretext was, that he had been compelled to fight the battle of Borghetto, because Venice had permitted the Austrians to occupy Peschiera, for which an indemnity was due.

If the Directory looked beyond, Bonaparte would keep open the quarrel, and seize a favourable moment to execute their designs. And while he thus wrote, he naively said that the "truth" was, that Beaulieu had deceived the Venetians, and had occupied Peschiera without their consent. Neutrality was no obstacle to him. We have seen that he not only held Peschiera but Verona, and the country round about.

Another work he completed was an armistice with Naples. This followed hard upon the defeat of the Austrians. By this convention, he separated the Neapolitan cavalry from Beaulieu's army, the Neapolitan ships of war from the English, and boasted that he had so arranged as to be able, at any moment, to make the Neapolitan horsemen prisoners.

Having awed the Venetians and detached the Neapolitans from the coalition, he completed the investment of Mantua. This fortress was at that time connected with the firm land by four causeways, each well defended. The melting of the snows had swollen all the streams, and augmented the water around Mantua. Bonaparte could not begin a regular siege for this and other reasons; and he, therefore, seized the head of each causeway, of which the most important was the Faubourg of St George.

From Mantua he departed for Milan, and thence by Pavia to Tortona. His business in this quarter was to suppress an irritating insurrection in the imperial fiefs, a work performed by Lannes with severity and decision. He shot, burned, and destroyed, in revenge for the assassination of Frenchmen. Every commune was directed to send two hostages to Tortona. The *seigneurs* were ordered to take the oath of obedience to the republic within five days, on pain of confiscation.

Each commune was to deposit its contribution within four-and-twenty hours, the contribution to be augmented by one-tenth for every day's delay. All found with arms after the publication of the order to be shot Every village which did not, in twenty-four hours, break the bells used to sound the tocsin was to be burned. At the same time, a fierce despatch was sent to the senate of Genoa. If they would not take measures to purge their territory of assassins, Bonaparte would take them—what kind of measures, we have already seen. "The French Republic is inviolably attached to the principle of neutrality, but the Republic of Genoa can no longer be the haunt of brigands." His quarrel with Genoa was studiously kept alive until a more favourable moment arrived for turning it to profit.

Bonaparte also regulated the conditions for carrying out the treaty of peace which the Directory had made with the King of Sardinia, whereby he secured all that he desired for the safety of his communications, and became, in fact, master of Piedmont

This work done, he directed Augereau to break up from Mantua and pass the Po, and he ordered a body of troops from the Adige to replace those marching with Augereau. The Directory, knowing nothing of war, had long been anxious to subject Rome, Naples, and Tuscany. Bonaparte, who knew what was impossible, had restrained their unbridled rapacity as much as he could; hence the armistice with Naples, But the wealth of the Pope offered too much temptation to republican virtue. He had money, arms, manuscripts, pictures—four things which inspired the armies of the republic with an "uncontrollable impulse." The Revolution had a real quarrel with the Pope; they were two extremes, but in this case extremes did not meet, except in collision.

Bonaparte, quitting. Tortona on the 17th of June, passed through Modena on the 19th, and on the 20th fixed his headquarters at Bologna. He instantly seized the Legates both at Bologna and Ferrara, and every other Papal authority of any importance. He took possession of the arms, munitions, and strong places. He sent Murat and Lannes to Reggio, and Vaubois to Pistoja, enjoining them to repress plundering with a heavy hand. He restored to the Bolognese the privileges which the Popes had taken away; but he exacted from the Senate, through his adjutant-general, that symbol of the independence conferred by the French on Italy—an oath of obedience to the French Republic. He seized heavy guns for the siege of Mantua wherever he could find them—at Fort Urban, at Modena, at Ferrara. By rapidity and pitiless vigour he so terrified the Papal Government, that the Pope gave to Chevalier d'Azara, Spanish Minister at Rome, authority to sign an armistice; and the deed was executed at Bologna, on the 23rd of June.

By this instrument the Pope agreed to liberate political prisoners, and restore their goods; to close his ports to the enemies of France, and open them to the French; to cede Bologna and Ferrara, and the citadel of Ancona; to deliver to the Republic a hundred pictures, busts, vases, or statues, among which should be the bronze bust of Junius Brutus and the marble bust of Marcus Brutus (a characteristic demand), and to give up five hundred manuscripts.

The Pope was likewise to pay 15,500,000 *livres* in cash, and 5,500,000 in provisions, merchandise, horses, cattle. This hard measure by no means represented the whole of the plunder: 4,000,000 *livres* were taken from Bologna, 3,000,000 from Ferrara, and 2,000,000 from Faenza; and, in addition to this, 4,700,000 were extorted in provisions and goods from the unhappy Legations. They paid a heavy price for liberty of swearing allegiance to Paris instead of to Rome. He demanded the treasures of Loretto, but met with such a lively opposition, that he accepted a million instead.

Quitting Bologna on the 23rd, he proceeded to Pistoja, and thence to Leghorn, where he arrived on the 27th. Here he heard the welcome news that Despinoy had at length compelled the stubborn Lamy to surrender the citadel of Milan,—a fortunate occurrence, which set free six or seven thousand men. He sent Lannes into Massa-Carara, to seize the property of the Government and the funds in the Mont de Piété, except sums under 200 *francs*; these were to be distributed to the people.

At Leghorn he took possession of all property belonging to English, Austrian, or Russian merchants; and he arrested the Governor of Leghorn because he favoured the English. Bonaparte, invited to Florence, proceeded thither and dined with the Grand Duke. He also, a little later, took measures for raising an insurrection in Corsica, then held by the English, whereby he got rid of the Commissary Salicetti, whom he sent to Corsica.

Bonaparte was well pleased with his rapid expedition to the south of the Po. At a cheap rate he humbled the Pope and the Grand Duke of Tuscany, and gave what he called liberty to the people of the Legations, who hated the Pope then as ardently as they hate him now; except those of Faenza, who, then as now, were Papal to the backbone. He obtained siege guns and small arms, great store of money, and much prestige. Writing from Bologna to the Directory, on the 2nd of July, he said—

> The artist commissaries whom you sent to the army have behaved very well, and are assiduous in their business. They have taken fifteen pictures from Parma, twenty from Modena, twenty-five from Milan, forty from Bologna, ten from Ferrara—110 in all. They have, besides, reaped an abundant harvest at Pavia, and we shall be much embarrassed by what we shall get at Rome.

Thus, Bonaparte reduced enemies who might have proved hurtful to silence and submission; armed his trenches at Mantua with their cannon; sent their works of art to embellish Paris; not only nourished his army and filled his military chest at their expense, but sent their gold and silver and precious stones to aid in filling the empty coffers at Paris, and in keeping on foot the French armies on the Rhine.

But it was time to return from this rapid promenade. Mantua was not taken; the armies on the Rhine were idle; and fresh Austrian troops were marching for the hills of the Tyrol; and a fresh general was about to strive with Bonaparte in the lists of war. Early in July, Bonaparte was once more on the northern bank of the Po.

CHAPTER 4

Bonaparte And Wurmser

While Bonaparte was engaged in the Genoese territory and the Legations, Massena kept a strict watch on Beaulieu, with some 14,000 men. His chief had placed under his command some of his best brigadiers, the accomplished Joubert, Rampon, daring and tenacious, and Victor, who, though sometimes too confident, was a good officer. At this time, of all his comrades in arms, Bonaparte had the highest opinion of Massena. In writing to the Directory, Bonaparte said of him that he was active, indefatigable; that he had audacity, *coup-d'œil,* and promptitude in deciding. Massena's task throughout June and July was to hold the forward position of Verona, and thus secure the line of the Adige.

In order to do this effectually, he placed his outposts on both sides of the Lake of Garda, and occupied the famous position of La Corona above Rivoli, between the Adige and the Monte Baldo. His headquarters were at Castiglione, where he could the better watch the roads on both sides of the lake down which Austrian columns might advance; and, during the interval of leisure allotted to the troops, he carefully attended to the drill and instruction of which some of them stood in need.

The Austrian General, Beaulieu, resigned his command when the Aulic Council sent Alvinzi to make inquiry into the causes of the disasters of the army, and pending the arrival of Wurmser, ordered from the Rhine, Melas took the command. This officer, while holding on strongly to the valley of the Adige, also posted battalions among the mountains from the Brenta to the frontiers of the Grisons. The Court of Vienna was determined to make a great effort to reinforce the army, raise the siege of Mantua, and do its uttermost to recover possession of Italy; and troops were marching from Germany and from the extreme frontiers of the empire to take part in the strife.

For six weeks Massena remained almost inactive. With a nominal force of 18,000 men, he had scarcely 13,000 under his immediate command. These men were almost as badly off as they were when on the rocks of Liguria. "No oats, no forage, no wine, no vinegar, no breeches, no coats, no shoes, no shirts," such were his repeated complaints to Berthier. These deficiencies were chiefly caused by the want of integrity and ability in the heads of the commissariat; and Bonaparte was frequently indignant that, in a country so rich, the civil department of the army would not manage to feed and clothe his men.

Rumours of the arrival of fresh troops kept Massena on the alert; and several small actions were fought at the advanced posts. Joubert surprised a partially entrenched position at the Bochetta de Campione, took 200 prisoners, some baggage and munitions. Recco, in like manner, surprised Belluno; but Victor was repulsed in an attack upon Malescnie, an Austrian camp on the lake of Garda. The great advantages which the French derived from the sojourn in this quarter was that they kept the enemy aloof from the country between the Mincio and Adige, used the opportunity of acquiring an accurate knowledge of a country, whereon, at a later date, Bonaparte displayed at its brightest his astonishing genius, and covered alike the communications with Milan, and the troops blockading and besieging Mantua.

Massena's position on the Adige was connected with the investing force at Mantua, through Villafranca and Roverbella. Bonaparte's expedition beyond the Po, and the want of heavy guns, had compelled Serurier's division to stand on the defensive. But the fell of the citadel of Milan and the capture of siege artillery made by Bonaparte in the Legations supplied the means for a siege, and the return of the chief himself gave the impulse. Early in July, then, the operations against Mantua took a more decisive character. It was time; for the Austrians were rapidly gathering in the Tyrol, and Massena anticipated an attack from day to day.

In 1796 the fortified place of Mantua differed little from what it is now. Standing on two islands of considerable size, in the midst of a lake formed by the Mincio, covered on the south by the vast marshes that stretch down to the Po, approachable only by narrow causeways, two of which serve as dykes to keep the upper lake full of water, Mantua was almost impregnable at that date, whatever it may be now.

All around the country is damp and pestiferous; and this is one reason why the Austrians of our day have made Verona their chief stronghold. As early as the 3rd June the French had seized the Faubourg of St. George, at the head of the causeway of that name, a post that played a great part in subsequent events. They had also seized the causeway leading from Cerese. When Bonaparte arrived, he pressed forward the labours of the siege with great vigour. He employed 7,000 men in the siege. Boats were armed with cannon, batteries were erected, trenches were opened; some advantages were gained over an enemy who offered a stout resistance on every side. Serurier, Dallemagne, Chasseloup, and Marat, inspired and led the French soldiers. Bonaparte knew that no time was to be lost

On the 6th of July he estimated his own force at 44,000, of whom some 5,000 were in hospital, and he estimated the enemy's army, including the garrison of Mantua, at 67,000 men; of whom 59,000 were in the field. He foresaw that his numbers would be diminished by disease, and he urged on his willing officers, carried his trenches nearer and nearer to the enemy's works, and frequently set fire to the town with shells and red-hot shot By the end of July the French had closed with the Austrian works, and were preparing for a final bombardment and assault, where a series of events in another quarter called away the general and his troops.

Wurmser had arrived in the Tyrol, He had with him, not as Bonaparte thought, nearly 60,000 men, but he had under his hands nearly 50,000, and about 200 guns, stretched out in a line from Vicenza to the head waters of the Lake of Iseo. Wurmser was a good soldier, and no contemptible opponent, but he was controlled by a staff sent to his headquarters by the Aulic Council, a fatal system of making war.

The French army, towards the end of July, was between the Western shore of the Lake of Garda and the right bank of the Adige. Augereau was at Legnago, on the Adige, with 8,000 men; Massena held Verona, Rivoli, and La Corona, with 13,000 men; Sauret, with some 5,000, was at Salo on the west of the Lake of Garda, covering the roads to Brescia and Lonato; the reserve was at Castiglione, Villafranca, and Castelnuovo. Bonaparte gave ample instructions and warnings to all his officers, and Berthier himself assiduously reconnoitred the left of the French position, between the Lake of Garda and the Adige.

Wurmser's plan was projected on a vast scale. He divided his army into three divisions, each separated from the other, and deprived of those rapid communications so essential to the success of combined attacks. Bonaparte's army was within his reach; even the division of Serurier at Mantua, as we shall see, arrived in time to secure a victory. But Wurmser split his army in two by the Lake of Garda, and thus, although he had superior numbers, like Beaulieu, he was destined, like Beaulieu, to be defeated in detail. His plan was this.

Quasdanowich, with 17,000 men, and forty guns, was directed to march by the west of the Lake of Garda, driving Sauret before him, and to occupy in succession Gavardo, Salo, Brescia, Montechiaro. He was, therefore, not only separated from the main army, but his columns were likely to become separated from each other. The centre, in two columns, 24,000 strong, with fifty guns, under Melas and Davidowich, was to descend the valley of the Adige on both banks, and effect a junction below Rivoli, drive the French from Verona, and cross the Mincio at Valeggio and Goito. Wurmser marched with his centre. On the left Mezaros, with 5,000 men and ten guns, was to march from Vicenza upon Verona, and expelling the French, join the centre.

The Austrian columns began their march on the morning of the 29th July. Bonaparte had not yet given a single order for the concentration of his troops, but they were all close at hand except Serurier. Melas crept upon the French post at Monte Baldo, surprised the advanced guard at dawn, and by a simultaneous movement attacked the position of Corona in front and flank. In vain Joubert sent reinforcements; they served only to arrest, but they did not stop the progress of the enemy; and when the Austrians descended from Monte Baldo upon the left of the entrenchments at Corona, the whole force, except 200 men, retired from the position.

Joubert now made a new effort both upon the Monte Baldo and the Corona; but the Austrians carried the redoubt, and the French were forced to fly. It is related of Joubert, always prompt to show an example of daring, that when he saw his men run from the redoubt, he entered with two men, overturned its two guns upon the enemy, and escaped amidst a storm of balls. The battalions placed higher up the Adige were cut off and taken.

Joubert fell back on Rivoli, and took post in the redoubt which had been constructed there by Massena during the six weeks of rest. Here he hoped to hold his ground. Massena promised reinforcements, sent Victor with 900 men, arrived himself with four guns, and reanimated his soldiers. Davidowich, who had marched down the left bank of the Adige, was now rapidly passing the river at Dolce, to take part in the combat. He had arrived at the defile of Incanale just as the French gunners, their ammunition failing, had spiked their pieces. Davidowich seized this favourable moment, rushed through the defile, and gained the right flank of Joubert, who instantly sent his guns to the rear, and throwing back his right, took a newer position, pivoting upon Victor. Melas followed his movements, but the night put an end to the combat. So far, the Austrian centre had been successful.

On the right, Quasdanowich moved forward in six columns against the posts held by the Frenchman, Sauret. He was most successful. His columns, descending the mountains, drove the

French from Salo and Gavardo, occupied these places, cut off General Guyeu with one battalion, blockaded him in an old castle, and forced Sauret to take post at Desenzano. On the left, however, Mezaros had made little progress, and had marched only to Montebello.

Bonaparte heard of his reverses on his road from Brescia to Peschiera. They did not daunt him. He halted at Montechiaro on the evening of the 29th, and dictated a host of orders. Augereau was called up from the Adige. Massena was directed to pass the Mincio at Peschiera, leaving a garrison there. Rampon was withdrawn from Verona. The need was so pressing, that Serurier was ordered to raise the siege of Mantua, abandon his cannon in the trenches, leave a garrison in the Faubourg of St. George, and hasten by forced marches by Macaria upon Castiglione.

The troops beyond the Po, except the garrison of Leghorn, were also recalled. In this moment, too, when he was scheming victory in his fertile brain, he was taking every precaution for a retreat And well might he cast a glance towards Cremona and Piacenza, when an enemy had seized Brescia, and had cut him off from Milan. One cannot but admire the daring, the decision, the soundness of Bonaparte's proceedings at this critical moment; and the coolness of head and clearness of eye which made him estimate the evil tidings which poured in at their true value, and led him to hope that, if fortune seconded his exertions, he should yet snatch a triumph from his divided foes.

On the 30th, Massena, Joubert, and Victor fell back fighting before the combined attacks of Melas and Davidowich; Mezaros entered Verona, which Rampon had quitted; and the column of Quasdanowich occupied Brescia, and seized Ponte San Marco on the Chiese. The column which surprised Brescia captured there three wounded generals, six brigadiers, some 1,400 sick and wounded, and between 200 and 300 soldiers. The Austrian star was still in the ascendant.

On the 31st, Wurmser debouched from the narrow way between the Adige and the Lake of Garda, and reached the Mincio, where his skirmishers fell in with the French, and kept up a fusillade. He was under the impression that Bonaparte had divided his forces, in imitation of his own movements; and that, while Massena contended with Quasdanowich, Bonaparte was posted at Roverbella, covering the siege of Mantua. This erroneous opinion induced him to march down the Mincio, and enter Mantua in triumph on the 1st August. But, during the time occupied in this useless promenade, events had happened which frustrated all his schemes. Bonaparte had united his whole army in rear of the Mincio, except the division of Serurier, swiftly marching up from Mantua.

Bonaparte made the most of the time so opportunely wasted by Wurmser. On the 31st he directed Sauret to carry Salo and release General Guyeu. Sauret executed the order with promptitude; and Guyeu, seconding his fierce onset by a sortie from the castle, joined him. Rusca, also made prisoner on the 29th, was delivered from the enemy. Sauret, however, was again compelled to fall back upon Desenzano. On the same day, General Ott fell upon the French posted at Lonato; but Dallemagne fought stoutly, and a sharp combat ended in the defeat of Ott, who retired across the Chiese, and regained Gavardo.

Augereau had arrived at Montechiaro on the 31st; and, on the 1st August, sending a detachment to dislodge an Austrian post from Ponte San Marco, he marched rapidly upon Brescia, and entered at one gate as the Austrians filed through another. Pressing on with characteristic impetuosity, he sent his cavalry in pursuit, and forced the enemy to seek shelter in the hills. He found all the magazines untouched; he recovered the prisoners, and the sick and wounded; and, what was of greater moment, the communications of the army with Milan were by this movement again in their possession.

There was still no time to lose. Wurmser was marching from Mantua, and Quasdanowich might at any moment renew his attempts to effect a junction with his chief. But the aspect of affairs was now far more favourable to Bonaparte. He had withdrawn Massena from the Mincio, and recalled Augereau from

Brescia to Montechiaro; he had secured his communications with Serurier, and he was once more fighting with a good road behind him. In fact, Bonaparte was in the position similar to that he occupied in his first advance upon the Mincio, but he had now the advantage afforded by the possession of Peschiera, which he had entrusted to the care of Guillaume, a staunch and valiant soldier.

Before Massena rejoined the main body, Quasdanowich, descending from Gavardo, drove Despinoy into Brescia, and continuing his movement in the hope of reaching his long-looked-for chief, met instead the advanced guard of Massena coming from Peschiera to Lonato. The Austrian general attacked briskly, and in the first onset took General Pijon prisoner, and captured three guns. But seeing that he stretched out his wings in the hope of surrounding the French, Massena and Bonaparte, skirmishing on their flanks, directed the weight of their forces in close column upon the enemy's centre, and threw him into confusion. early in the day, Bonaparte had directed General Guyeu to seize Salo.

Quasdanowich had given the same order to one of his brigadiers. The latter arrived first at Salo, and, finding no enemy, withdrew, Salo, therefore, was occupied by Guyeu. This proved a piece of good fortune; for Quasdanowich, defeated at Lonato, retreated by the road from Desenzano to Salo, vigorously pursued by Junot with the French cavalry. Cut off at Salo, nearly the whole of one brigade of Austrians threw down their arms. This was the finishing stroke to Quasdanowich, who, nevertheless, still remained at Gavardo.

The French officer, Valette, had abandoned Castiglione on the 2nd of August, although he had been ordered to defend it to the last Bonaparte immediately cashiered him. His cowardice caused a serious combat. During the action of the 3rd, Augereau was compelled to assail the advanced guard of Wurmser at Castiglione, and maintain the fight there all day against considerable odds. He did so, with various fortune—now driven back, now making head, but finally prevailing. Wurmser's troops, coming from the Mincio, augmented hourly; but the French, masters of Lonato, were able to act on the rear of their enemies, who, seduced by a feigned retreat, advanced too far towards Montechiaro, and gave Kilmaine's horse time to arrive and take a brilliant part in the fight.

On the French side, Beyrand was killed, and Augereau and several superior officers more or less seriously wounded. But they took several thousand prisoners, and killed or wounded 2,000 or 3,000 men in the double combat fought that day. The French were between two bodies of the enemy; but they obstructed the larger with a lesser force, and routed the smaller with the bulk of the army.

Wurmser, now thoroughly awake to his position, rallied the greater party of his army in a position between Solferino and Monte Medolano. But he still had detachments engaged in separate operations, On the 4th, while the Austrian was gathering up his columns, Bonaparte, anxious to remove Quasdanowich from his rear, ordered Despinoy to move from Brescia upon Gavardo, in concert with Dallemagne at Rezzato, and Guyeu at Salo. The operation was successful, although Despinoy failed and carried off part of his troops in the midst of the engagement The enemy were surprised, and driven across the Chiese; several hundred prisoners were taken, and two battalions, commanded by a Colonel Knor, were cut off. Instead of surrendering, they resolved to fight their way through the French right and join Wurmser, if possible, at Castiglione.

In consequence whereof, a strange adventure happened to Bonaparte, which may best be told in his own words.

"During the day," he says, "I went to Lonato to see what troops could be drawn from there. But what was my surprise, on entering the place, to receive the bearer of a flag of truce, who summoned the commander of Lonato to surrender, because, said the fellow, he was surrounded on all sides. And really, *videttes* rode in, announcing that various columns touched our grand guards, and that the route to Brescia was intercepted at the Pont San Marco. I felt then that these troops could only be the wreck of the division cut off at Gavardo, which, having assembled, was endeavouring to cut for itself a passage to the Mincio.

"This was rather embarrassing. I had only 1,200 men at Lonato. I therefore caused the envoy to be brought into my presence, and the bandage to be taken from his eyes. I told him, that if his General had the presumption to capture the commander-in-chief of the army of Italy, he had only to advance; that he ought to be aware that I was at Lonato, since all the world knew my army was there; that all the general officers of his division should be responsible for the personal insult he had offered. I declared to him, that if in eight minutes his division had not piled arms, I would not pardon one of them. The envoy seemed extremely astonished to find me there, and soon after the whole of the column piled its arms. It was 4,000 strong,, had two pieces of cannon, and fifty cavalry soldiers. It came from Gavardo, and sought an issue to save itself by Lonato."

This anecdote is pretty well authenticated; but Bonaparte, as usual, has greatly exaggerated the strength of the column. He does not, however, tell us one curious fact, reported by General Koch, that the envoy had hardly quitted his presence ere Bonaparte galloped past him, and, spurring his horse into the midst of the column, himself commanded them to lay down their arms.

Quasdanowich beaten out of the field, Bonaparte prepared to fight Wurmser, who, although he had failed to effect a junction with his right wing, and had suffered severely in the double action on the 3rd, laid siege to Peschiera, and posted the bulk of his army, 25,000 strong, between Castiglione and the Mincio. He directed Mezaros, who was on the lower Po, in conjunction with the Governor of Mantua, to drive Fiorella, commanding part of Serurier's division, across the Oglio. The Governor could lend him no aid, and Fiorella defeated Mezaros. Thus Wurmser was deprived of the corps of Mezaros, and the force blockading Peschiera.

The Austrian position had Castiglione in front, and the Mincio a few miles in the rear. Wurmser covered the points of passage at Valeggio, Goito, and Ponti. His right was at Solferino on high ground; his left at Medolane, and a redoubt on a hillock protected this flank. Bonaparte had united the divisions of Augereau and Massena in front of Castiglione.

Gardanne, who commanded the brigades of Serurier's division coming from Marcaria, was ordered to march with all speed by Guidizzolo upon the left rear of the Austrian line. It should be borne in mind that Wurmser acted in the belief that Mezaros had disposed of Gardanne, and he therefore readily accepted battle when he might easily have crossed the Mincio.

The plan of the French general was to assail the Austrian right in such a manner as to lead Wurmser to give his whole attention on that side. For this purpose Massena made a great show of attacking Solferino. Wurmser easily pushed back the opposing skirmishers; and intent on victory on the flank where he still hoped to see the leading brigades of Quasdanowich, he extended his right with the view of outflanking Massena. Having so far misled his opponent, Bonaparte, spying the advanced guard of Gardanne at Guidizzolo, developed the real attack upon the Austrian left.

Marmont, then *aide-de-camp* to the commander-in-chief, and acting under his immediate orders, planted a battery of twelve guns at an oblique angle, raking the Austrian left. Beaumont, with his horse, charged their battalions, and wheeled into their left rear towards San Cassiano; while Verdier, and Joubert who had risen from a sick bed, stormed the redoubt at Medolane. Wurmser, seeing this pronounced assault on his left, halted his right brigades marching to outflank Massena; but it was too late. Gardanne was now upon the field in rear of his left; and he was compelled to use his reserve to face this unlooked-for and dangerous foe. The decisive moment had arrived. Wurmser was alike out-manoeuvred and out-numbered. The masterly combination of his opponent had succeeded. The battle was lost.

Bonaparte seized the golden moment for which he had waited impatiently—one of those moments which come once and but once in great battles. Augereau's hardy soldiers were sent headlong against the Austrian centre; Massena's men, who had to avenge their defeats on the Corona and at Rivoli, pressed in between the centre and right. The left was well handled by Beaumont and Gardanne, Wurmser, unwilling to retreat, made head for some time as well as he could against the raging storm; but when a body of fresh troops under Leclerc, which Bonaparte had called up from Brescia, entered the line, and, dashing at the tower of Solferino, carried it by main strength; and when Massena, breaking in between the right and centre, doubled his speed, to anticipate the Austrians at the bridge of Borghetto, Wurmser reluctantly gave orders to retreat

Happily for him, the brigade blockading Peschiera had marched towards the battlefield, guided by the thunder of the cannonade, and it arrived in time to protect the retreat of the right and part of the centre. The left, falling back before the impetuous onsets of Gardanne, Beaumont, and Augereau, reached the bridge of Borghetto. At the close of the day the Austrian right filed over the Mincio below Peschiera, and the other portion of the army entered Valeggio. The French were masters of the right bank of the river from Volta to the lake of Garda. They had taken 1,000 men, killed and wounded some 2,000, and captured nearly twenty guns during the day.

"Thus," wrote Bonaparte to the Directory, on the day after the battle, "another campaign has been finished in five days."

Once more an Austrian army was behind the Mincio. Again the General in command extended his troops, who were too few in number to occupy a line reaching from Peschiera to Mantua. He guarded the bridges which he did not break, and laboured hard to establish an entrenched camp near Peschiera. Again Bonaparte determined to break through without delay. The French army was on the scene of its earlier triumphs, and its general knew how to cross the Mincio. On the 6th, Augereau was sent against Valeggio; and Massena, traversing Peschiera, was ordered to storm and destroy the entrenched camp.

While Augereau cannonaded the enemy at Valeggio, Massena assailed the camp. Twice he was repulsed, but the third time, amply reinforced, he stormed the works, and drove their defenders upon Cavalcaselle. This victory opened to the French the road to the Tyrol. Bonaparte ordered Augereau to march up the left bank of the Mincio as far as Peschiera, leaving only a post at Borghetto.

But Wurmser, seeing his line of retreat menaced, although he was as desirous to prolong the period during which the magazines of Mantua might be replenished, as Bonaparte was to prevent him, yet he could not hold the line of the Mincio a moment after the French, masters of Peschiera, could unite their whole force and place it across the road to the Tyrol. Wherefore, on the night of the 6th, he retreated up the valley of the Adige while there was yet time, and halted only when he had reached the crests of Montebaldo, the heights of Corona, and the left bank of the Adige at Chiusa. Quasdanowich had also fallen back into a line with the main body.

The French generals followed the enemy at speed. They reached Verona before the rear-guard had quitted that city. The Venetian Governor refused to open the gates, and Bonaparte, not brooking delay, caused Dommartin to break down a gate with cannon shot, and entered before the enemy could escape. Mezaros was pursued on the road to Vicenza, but Davidowich escaped up the Adige as far as Dolce and Ala. Massena re-established his troops at Rivoli; Augereau occupied Verona, and watched the course of the Adige as far as Legnago; while Fiorella, replacing Serurier, who had fallen ill, renewed the blockade of Mantua; but, losing health himself, Sahuguet obtained the command. Mantua was now well provisioned, strongly garrisoned, and in communication with the Po and the Oglio.

Bonaparte now determined to wrest from the Austrians all the positions on the Adige and the Garda Lake, whence they could debouch upon Brescia and Verona. He, therefore, gave Sauret, who was at Salo, *carte blanche*; and this officer, in concert with St. Hilaire, drove the rear-guard of Quasdanowich from the defiles on both banks of the Chiese—took the Rocca d'Anfo, a small but strong fort—compelled the Prince de Reuss to seek safety in Trent, and took post with 5,000 men at Lodrone. Massena seized the defile of Incanale, the bridge of Chiusa, the Corona, Montebaldo, and Preabocco.

Augereau, marching up the left bank of the river in two columns, forced the enemy back to Roveredo and Trent. Thus, the two armies had returned to nearly the same positions which they had occupied when, a fortnight before, Wurmser pressed down from the mountains to raise the siege of Mantua. The French estimate their own loss, between the 29th of July and the 13th of August, at 6,000 killed or wounded, and 4,000 prisoners; and they estimate the loss of the Austrians at upwards of 16,000 men killed, wounded, or prisoners. "The Austrian army," said Bonaparte, "which for six weeks menaced Italy with invasion, had disappeared like a dream."

In the middle of August, the Austrians were between Trent and Bassano; and they still had more men than Bonaparte. The French were between the head of the Lake Iseo, and the right bank of the Adige in front of the Corona, with reserves in the rear at Rivoli. The right was at Verona.

During this brief campaign, Bonaparte looked anxiously for symptoms of revolt in his rear. He admitted that the Dukes of Parma and Tuscany, the people of Milan, Bologna, and Ferrara had behaved well; but he did not like the attitude of the Pope, the King of Naples, and the Senate of Venice.

"The people of Bologna, Ferrara, and especially Milan," he wrote to the Directory, on the 16th of August, "have, during our retreat, shown the greatest courage and attachment to liberty. At Milan, when it was said that the enemy was at Cassano, and we were flying, the people demanded arms, and one heard in the streets, in the squares, at the theatre, the martial air—'Allons enfants de la patrie!' The people of Casal-Maggiore, on the contrary, have taken arms, plundered our baggage, and slaughtered our sick.

At Castelnuovo, in the Venetian country, a volunteer was assassinated. I caused the house to be burnt, and inscribed on the ruins these words —'*Here a Frenchman was assassinated.*'"

Yet, a few days later, he issued a proclamation, directing that every Bolognese, wearing a foreign cockade, should be imprisoned; every stranger wearing a foreign cockade, subjected to a severer penalty; and all persons not respectful to the authorities were to be imprisoned or expelled.

Bonaparte's mode of dealing with the towns of Italy is illustrated by his proclamation to the authorities of Brescia on the 12th of August

"Two thousand sick Frenchmen and Austrians," he said, "are in the streets of Brescia; humanity ordains that they should be assisted. I order that three hundred may be placed in each convent. See that they are cared for and treated as they should be. The sick in the hospitals of Brescia stand in need of everything. During the day, you must procure for them every possible aid: necessity, humanity, religion so ordains. Therefore, you must furnish, during the day, to the Director-General of Hospitals, three thousand ells of lint, thirty thousand pints of good wine, ten puncheons of vinegar, fifteen hundred pints of brandy, two thousand pounds of sugar, three thousand lemons, and six thousand shirts. These things, like all else furnished by the town of Brescia, will be paid for; but it is indispensable that they should be furnished today. In default, I will impose upon Brescia a tax of 3,000,000 *livres*; and I shall be obliged to take what you do not furnish."

Brescia had shown no indisposition to the French. Casal-Maggiore is mentioned by the General as one of the places which behaved ill during his retreat He, therefore, levied in that place a million in contributions; obliged the people to indemnify the officers whose baggage they had taken, and transport, at their own expense, all their church bells to Alessandria. The guilty were to be judged by a military commission.

During the remainder of the month of August, Bonaparte was occupied in putting his army in better trim, and endeavouring to restore tranquillity on the line of his communications. In the first object he did not succeed very well. His efforts to feed the troops with regularity, and provide proper accommodation for his sick, were vitiated or frustrated by the civil commissaries appointed at Paris by political partisans, and more intent on filling their own pockets than on serving the public.

In vain Bonaparte gave orders—he was only half obeyed; and, although towards the end of August he had 15,000 sick, and suffered a loss of twenty men per day, he could not obtain what was needful either for the sick or the sound. As a natural consequence, the soldiers plundered on all sides, and the popularity which the army gained by its astonishing marches and victories was destroyed by the habit of marauding on the part of the common soldiers, and of imposing arbitrary contributions on the part of officers. Bonaparte hated disorder. He had no sentimental objection to the system of requisitions and contributions, but it must be carried out by his order; all else was plunder.

At this time he had his enemies in Paris. The journals criticised him somewhat rudely, and neither then nor in after life did he love criticism. He was hurt that men should think him ambitious; and, perhaps, at that time he really was less insincere in his opinion of constitutional liberty than he was a few years later. A letter to Carnot, written at Verona on the 9th of August, shows him in the light of one defending himself from unfair imputations, and is interesting for many reasons. No Bonaparte has ever spared professions.

"If," he says, "there is in France a single man, pure and of good faith, who can suspect my political intentions, and throw doubts upon my conduct, I renounce at this instant even the happiness of serving my country. Three or four months of obscurity will calm envy, re-establish my health, and place me in a position to occupy with more advantage the posts that the Government may confide to me. It was only by quitting Paris in time that I have been able to render great services to the Republic. When the moment comes, it will be only by quitting the army of Italy in time that I can consecrate the rest of my life to the Republic. The grand art of Government should be, not to allow men to grow old. I have adopted, in entering on my political career, as a principle—*all* for my country."

While engaged in refitting his troops, keeping Rome, Naples, and Venice in awe, organizing an expedition against the English in Corsica, preparing a mine in Genoese politics for future use, blockading Mantua, and turning keen glances upon the Brenta and Upper Adige, Bonaparte did not forget the brave mountaineers of the Tyrol. He did not assume for them, as for the people of Italy, that they desired to be free from Austria, that they might accept the liberty which was implied in an oath of allegiance to the French Republic; he knew better. But as the harbinger of a possible campaign through their country, he sent among the Tyrolese this proclamation, which breathes the spirit of *brigandage* rather than war:—

Inhabitants of the Tyrol! you solicit the protection of the French army; you must render yourselves worthy of it. Since the majority among you are well-intentioned, compel the obstinate few to submit. Their mad conduct only tends to draw the furies of war upon your country.

The superiority of the arms of France is now proved. The Ministers of the Emperor, bought by British gold, betray him: this unfortunate prince has not taken a step that is not a fault. You desire peace: the French fight for peace. We shall only enter your territory in order to oblige the Court of Vienna to submit to the desires of desolated Europe, and to hear the cries of its people. We do not come to aggrandize ourselves; nature has traced our limits on the Rhine and the Alps, as she has placed in the Tyrol the limits of the House of Austria.

Tyrolese! whatever may have been your past conduct, return to your homes; quit a flag so many times beaten, and powerless to defend your houses. It is not a few enemies the more that can frighten the conquerors of the Alps and Italy; but it is a few victims the less that the generosity of my nation orders me to endeavour to spare.

We have shown ourselves formidable in combat; but we are the friends of those who receive us with hospitality. The religion, customs, property of those who submit shall be respected. But those communes whose companies have not returned home when we arrive, shall be burned; their inhabitants shall be taken as hostages and sent to France. When a commune has submitted, the syndic shall instantly give up a note of those inhabitants who are in the pay of the Emperor; and if they are part of the companies of Tyrolese, their houses shall be burned, and their parents, to the third degree, arrested and sent as hostages to France. Every Tyrolese, belonging to a free company, taken with arms in his hands, shall be shot there and then.

The generals of divisions are charged with the strict execution of these orders.

But the Tyrolese were not daunted by these fulminating documents, and they had no trust in the promises of invaders.

CHAPTER 5

Wurmser's Second Campaign

The operations of Bonaparte were to a great extent depend-ent upon the campaign conducted by Jourdan and Moreau on the frontiers of Germany. These generals were at first completely successful, but their movements were divergent and badly com-bined; and at the end of September, the Archduke Charles, Aus-tria's best general, had defeated Jourdan in two pitched battles, and forced him back across the Rhine. Moreau had advanced nearly to Munich, when, hearing of the retreat of Jourdan, he was compelled to face about, retreat himself through the Black Forest, and pass the Rhine at Huninguen.

Now Bonaparte anticipated that Moreau, according to a pre-concerted plan, would march upon Innspruck, and thus force Davidowich, who held Trent, to retire. After waiting sometime in the vain expectation of receiving news of Moreau, Bonaparte determined to resume the offensive. He knew that Wurmser had occupied the line of the Brenta, and he divined his plan of op-erations.

On the 2nd of September he wrote to Berthier, that he was about to enter the Tyrol; that the enemy was at Bassano, and that it might happen, although it did not seem probable, that Wur-mser would be foolish enough to move on Verona and Porto-Legnago, pass the Adige, and endeavour to raise the blockade of Mantua. If Wurmser committed this folly, he should make him repent it; and Bonaparte's measures were, therefore, so taken as to be beforehand with the foe. At the same time he made every arrangement to prevent a disaster, in case, contrary to expectation, the Austrian general should succeed in seizing Verona.

Seeing that Wurmser had again divided his force, Bonaparte prepared to anticipate him, both on the Adige and the Brenta. He resolved to be first in the field, and crushing Davidowich, seize his line of communication, and march at once upon Bassano. His earliest care was to establish ample magazines. Then he caused the flotilla on the Lake of Garda to be collected, in order that Guyeu might embark his troops at Salo, and reach Torbole at the head of the lake, while Vaubois, who had succeeded Sauret, arrived with the whole of his division at the same place, and at the same time.

From Torbole Vaubois was directed to march upon Roveredo, in the valley of the Adige. Massena received orders to march at mid-day, on the 2nd September, with the whole of his division upon Ala, on the left bank of the Adige, keeping good watch on the right bank, and guarding his bridge at Polo. Augereau was to march at the same time from Verona, through the hills, and take post on the road from Verona to Roveredo and between Lago and Rovere. Kilmaine was directed to cover Verona, patrol as far as Vicenza, and keep a grand guard of cavalry at Legnago. Thus Bonaparte had directed three divisions against the weaker half of Wurmser's army.

Wurmser hoped that Bonaparte would enter the Tyrol and follow Davidowich, while he, moving across the Adige, fell upon the rear of the French, entangled in the defiles, and ensured their destruction. Bonaparte was, however, too quick for him, and while Wurmser lingered about Bassano, the French General was in the midst of the quarters of the Austrian right wing.

The only chance against Bonaparte was involved in the march of Vaubois upon a separate line; but even in this fortune favoured him. On the 3rd September Massena had reached Ala, and Bonaparte fixed there his headquarters for the night. Augereau was ordered to march with the dawn from his position upon Roveredo. The cavalry were brought up to that place; and Vaubois, informed of the movements on the Adige, was directed to detach a corps to secure his communication with the main body, from which Marmont was sent with a cavalry patrol to feel for Vaubois.

The advanced posts of the Austrians were commanded by Wukassowich, whom the reader will recognize as the officer who so nearly retrieved the loss of the first combat at Dego. He fell back fighting upon San Marco. He had vainly besought assistance. Wurmser and Davidowich were far from the front, engaged in laying plans for the destruction of the French. Assailed on the 4th at San Marco, Wukassowich made head for two hours against his adventurous enemy; but at length he was overpowered, turned, and forced to retire upon Roveredo.

Dubois, hurried up with the horse, charged the flying enemy, and met a soldier's death at the head of his men. Vaubois, on his side, had forced the entrenched camp at Mori, and continued his advance on a parallel front to that of Massena. Augereau guarded the right flank, and was held in readiness to seize the line of communication between Trent and Bassano.

The day was yet young when the Austrians, in several columns retired, and Bonaparte determined to follow up his blow. Rampon, therefore, turned the Austrian right by pressing between Roveredo and the Adige, while Victor charged into the main streets, slew many of the enemy, and expelled him from the town. The Austrians retired towards Caliano, and took a strong position between the steep mountains and the Adige. Here they were reinforced, and brought their artillery into play. But nothing could stop the French. Employing his cannon to shake the Austrian column in the ravine, Bonaparte sent Pijon up the heights on the right, some hundreds of skirmishers on the left, and caused a squadron of hussars to charge the Austrians.

These measures were completely successful. The hussars charged right through the column, and wheeling round fell on the rear, while the infantry redoubled its attacks on the front and flanks. The result was, that part of the Austrians retreated, 6,000 men laid down their arms, twenty-five guns and seven flags were captured. Such was the battle of Roveredo; it secured the success of Bonaparte's plan.

During the night after the battle, a singular adventure befell General Leclerc. Vaubois was still on the right bank of the Adige, and Leclerc, ordered to search for him, fell into the hands of an Austrian patrol. Finding that he did not return, Desaix set out with an escort of eight men, and by a happy chance encountered the captors. Challenged, the Austrians fired, and shot dead a Frenchman, whereupon Desaix, who never wanted presence of mind, thundered out—"First battalion, forward, march!" and riding on, at once summoned the Austrians to surrender. His daring and ready wit were rewarded by the release of Leclerc, and the capture of the Austrian patrol.

Davidowich retired through Trent. Vaubois crossed the Adige; and with two divisions Bonaparte entered Trent early on the 5th. Losing no time, he ordered Augereau to march as fast as he could upon Levico, a position in the valley of Sugana, where he would be master of the road from Trent on the Adige, to Bassano on the Brenta, and to continue his movement on the 6th down the river. Vaubois was sent forward to dislodge Davidowich from a strong post he had occupied at Lavis, behind the Avisio. The combat was sharp for a time; and one attack was repulsed; but the resolute march of Dallemagne, and the dashing energy of Murat, carried all before them. Davidowich was hurled back on the road to Botzen, and rendered quite harmless for the present.

Wurmser had sent forward his leading columns, and they were in full march down the Brenta when he heard of the forward movement of Bonaparte. As this was what he looked for, he only hastened his troops. But he was soon undeceived. The French came storming up the valley of the Adige faster than the waters flowed down; and before the veteran Alsatian could re-assemble his army, Bonaparte was actually on the right flank of his column of march, and racing after him towards Bassano. Vaubois was left at Trent to guard that route, but every other soldier, even part of Vaubois' corps, was turned to the right down the valley of the Brenta.

Wurmser on the evening of the 6th had one division at Vicenza, a second at Bassano, and a third at Primolano, eighteen miles from his centre. He was still full of his project; but he had soon to repent. Bonaparte pressed the march of his columns, and at dawn on the 7th overtook the rear guard of the division under Quasdanowich, at Primolano and the tower of Covolo. Augereau attacked the post with great rapidity. Charging the front with a close column, he carried Primolano, and kept up the fight until the position was turned and Covolo stormed through an embrasure. The Austrians retreated; but being followed, and charged by the cavalry, five guns were taken, and 2,000 men threw down their arms. In this brilliant action the French had a great superiority of force.

On the 8th, at daybreak, Bonaparte renewed his march. He had before him the defiles of the Brenta, but he knew that if he were quick enough, he should find them guarded by an inferior force. And so it turned out. Wurmser had posted two or three weak brigades at the villages in the gorge, and had united the rest of his army at Bassano, the corps of Mezaros excepted, which, in happy ignorance, was inarching on Verona. Bonaparte, eager to reap the fruits of his brilliant strategy and rapid marches, moved at two in the morning from Cismone, and, acting on both banks of the river, turned the positions of the enemy, and took many prisoners, including the two commanders of the brigades.

The combat ended, the French resumed their march, and arriving before Bassano ere Wurmser had completed his preparations for defence, and attacking swiftly from both sides of the Brenta, they carried the town and the camp, split the whole force into sections, captured 3,000 prisoners, and upwards of thirty guns, drove Quasdanowich towards Treviso, and Wurmser, by Cittadella, to Vicenza. The Austrian army was now in three parts. Davidowich had been forced northwards, into the heart of the Tyrol; Quasdanowich was flying to the eastward; and Wurmser had gone towards the Adige.

"In six days," wrote Bonaparte in the exultation of triumph, "we have fought two battles and four combats. We have taken from the enemy twenty-one colours; we have made 16,000 prisoners, among whom are many generals; the rest have been killed, wounded, or scattered abroad. We have, in six days, always fighting in inexpugnable gorges, marched five-and-forty leagues, taken seventy pieces of cannon, with their caissons, their horses, a part of their grand park, and considerable magazines spread along the route."

We cannot take all this for granted; but, although inaccurate, it gives a vivid idea of the fiery rapidity with which he had fallen among and cut asunder his foes.

Wurmser, cut off from all communication with Germany, took the bold course of marching upon Mantua. Bonaparte, on the 9th, directed Augereau upon Padua, and laid Massena on the heels of the Austrians. The French entered Vicenza on the 9th, and there Bonaparte wrote to Augereau, ordering him to go with all speed to Legnago, and he instructed Sahuguet, who was blockading Mantua, to occupy certain specified points, in order that Wurmser might be cut off.

On the evening of the 10th Massena crossed the Adige at Ronco; but Augereau, although he forced a march, arrived too late at Legnago. Wurmser was on the right bank, and the place was held by a detachment. Massena marched rapidly towards Sanguinetto, to cut off Wurmser, but he was misled; General Ott defeated his advanced guard with great spirit, and drove it back towards Ronco. The Austrians were now saved. Augereau was detained before Legnago; Massena had been repulsed; Sahuguet had failed to execute the orders of his chief; and Wurmser, overthrowing the small detachments he accidentally encountered, arrived in safety in Mantua.

On the 13th Augereau had induced the Governor of Legnago to capitulate; the garrison to lay down their arms, withdraw to Trieste, and serve no more during the war. This obstacle removed, Bonaparte could again take measures for blockading Mantua.

The garrison of Mantua, reinforced by 5,000 or 6,000 men,

was not disposed to submit tamely to a close blockade. Wurmser took a position outside the place, in front of the Faubourg of St. George, with an advanced post at the village of Due Castelli. Massena, coming from Castellaro on the 14th, surprised the outpost, and carried the village. The French, too elated with their success, advanced in loose order, and Austrian reinforcements, both foot and horse, arriving, the French were quickly driven back, and brilliantly repulsed.

Bonaparte, piqued in his turn, arranged a combined attack for the 15th. Sahuguet was directed to move down the Roverbella road upon the left wing of the Austrians. Seldom fortunate in war, he was at first repulsed with loss, but; bringing up his whole force, he compelled the Austrians to retire into the palace, called La Favorite. Augereau, in the meantime, was moving up the left bank of the Mincio from Governolo, upon the right flank of the Austrians, and, reaching St. George's, he instantly attacked. In order to repel this formidable movement, Wurmser employed part of the battalions in the centre of his line.

Attacked anew by Sahuguet in his position at La Favorite, Wurmser sent a reinforcement from the centre to that wing also. Bonaparte, who had kept Massena in reserve and out of view, seized this moment to strike at the weakened centre. Victor, Chabran, Rampon, gallantly leading their men, broke in upon the Faubourg in front and flank, and the right wing hearing the fierce storm of cannon and musketry in their rear, gave way before the assaults of Augereau. In their course they came upon two French battalions belonging to Sahuguet's division, which were on the causeway leading from St. George's to the citadel. Sahuguet had not been quick enough with his supports; but Rampon, the hero of Monte Legino, seeing the danger of the two battalions, led his regiment into the fray, and the Austrians were slain, driven into the water, captured, or forced into the place. Wurmser was now shut up in the fortress which he had marched to save.

In this action both sides lost great numbers of men, but the Austrians the greater. The French also captured twenty-five guns, and once more resumed possession of the most favourable positions for making the blockade effective.

Once more the army of Italy had an interval of comparative rest. One strong division remained around Mantua, breathing the foul exhalations of its marshes, and performing the cheerless and irksome duties of a blockading force. Bonaparte fairly shut up Wurmser in his pestiferous prison, and entrusted to Kilmaine the task of keeping him there. Vaubois was sent into the Tyrol to watch the valley of the Adige with 8,000; Augereau and Massena were ordered first to Verona, and afterwards to the Brenta. The aggregate of these forces was between 12,000 and 14,000 men.

Bonaparte betook himself to Milan on the 19th of September, and remained there until the 12th of October, when he crossed the Po, to settle the affairs of Modena, the Legations, and Rome. By the 23rd of October he was again at Verona, preparing for a strife which he foresaw would soon be renewed. In this interval he gave himself up to politics, an inquiry into the civil administration of the army, and preparations for the future.

He had to keep the Pope in a state of salutary awe of his, soldiers, and to counterwork the intrigues of Rome, which ramified all around him. When Wurmser made his second stroke for victory, the Italian powers showed strong symptoms of throwing off the French yoke; and the Pope was foremost among them. But Bonaparte, while he arrested the Legates and rebuked them, bidding them as priests not to meddle in politics, had no desire to break with Rome at that moment.

All his efforts at Paris and Rome were directed to keep the peace; to bully and wheedle the Papal Court, and to show the Directory the madness of making war with everybody at once. He desired to eat one at a time. He advised the Directory to make peace with Naples, and to keep Rome in the toils of a negotiation or an armistice, until the moment came to march upon that "superb city." The Directory took his advice in both cases; made peace with Naples, and kept up delusive negotiations with Rome.

Another business on hand was the manufacture of a revolution in Modena. The duke had a minister at Paris negotiating a peace. Bonaparte advised the Directory to tell the duke's envoy that their general in Italy had been charged with the making of peace, in order that the said general might—not make peace—but choose his own time for breaking altogether with the regency left behind by the duke. This plot was transacted successfully.

When the duke's envoy went to Milan, he was placed under arrest, and cut off from all communication with the world; Bonaparte declared the armistice to be at an end, and took the people of Reggio and Modena under the protection of the French Republic. Thus, as Bonaparte said, the Directory had Modena, Reggio, Bologna, Ferrara, all "under one nightcap;" the people united in a congress, executed his behests, and grew every day "more fitted for liberty:" "the majority," he wrote, "regard us as liberators, and our cause as their cause."

He opposed the fanaticism of the revolution to the fanaticism of Rome. He allowed them to raise a Lombard Legion and Italian Legion; and as the tricolour was the favourite combination, they adopted for the national colours the now famous white, red, and green. Bonaparte took care that these legions were officered by Frenchmen or Italians devoted to France, and he proposed to employ them or some of them in the blockade of Mantua.

Piedmont was a source of great trouble. No cordial relations could be maintained between the two countries. Bonaparte was anxious touching the course of Piedmont His line of communications was at the mercy of bands of guerrillas, who infested the road by the Col de Tenda, slew his couriers, assassinated General Dujard, plundered his convoys. He wrote fierce despatches, demanded an indemnity, and the destruction of the brigands, who, he averred, were protected and encouraged by the authorities at Turin. But at bottom he desired an offensive and defensive alliance with Piedmont, a consummation for which he had to wait until his victories made it no longer possible for Piedmont to resist.

Venice, also, attracted his attention. He looked with suspicion upon her armaments and nursed the pretexts of a quarrel, while he strove to awe the Senate and maintain peaceful relations. He spoke to the Italian Courts through the democrats of Modena and the Legations, whom he had under his "nightcap."

"Woe to those who draw down the wrath of the French army," he wrote to the Bolognese. "Woe to Ravenna, Faenza, Rimini, if ever, misled into error, they fail in the respect they owe to the victorious French army, and the friends of the liberty of every people! . . . . The time has come when Italy is about to show herself with honour among powerful nations. Lombardy, Bologna, Modena, Reggio, Ferrara, perhaps Romagna, if she prove worthy, will one day astonish Europe, and retrace for us the noblest days of Italy. Rush to arms! The portion of Italy which is free is populous and rich. Make the enemies of your rights and liberties tremble. I shall not lose sight of you. The republicans will show you the road to victory, and teach you how to beat the tyrants, I will direct your battalions, and your happiness will be in part your own work. Tell those madmen who brave the anger of France, that she protects the nations and religion; but that, for the arrogant who brave her, she is terrible as the exterminating angel."

It is impossible not to admire the profound political tactics of Bonaparte, who, while maintaining the Italians completely under his thumb or nightcap, amused them with the show of freedom, and turned their passions against his foes.

Failing to obtain an alliance with Piedmont, he urged the Directory to insist on an alliance with Genoa. Bonaparte had long been engaged in a line of policy tending to frighten the Genoese. At one time he talked of marching against them; at another, he preferred fierce complaints to the Senate; then he dissimulated, and suspended his measures. Finally, the Directory took the matter in hand. Bonaparte was solely animated by a desire to secure a line of retreat in case of need, and a line of communication, out of the reach of the ill-will, which, in spite of all his efforts, he knew that the Court of Turin justly felt towards one who had reduced it so low.

His hopes were at length fulfilled. The *"oligarchs"* were made to suffer in pocket and position. On the 9th of October, a treaty was signed, stipulating for the payment of 4,000,000 *livres*, the closing of the port against the English, and the free passage of the troops and convoys destined for the army of Italy. This treaty, to use the language of Jomini, transformed Genoa into a French place of arms; precisely what Bonaparte desired, and what he had been for many months intriguing to effect.

Another task, which he undertook while at Milan, was the overhauling of the financial administration.

"Since I have been at Milan," he writes on the 12th of October, "I have employed myself in making war upon rogues. As long as I have your confidence, I will wage a pitiless war upon thieves and Austrians."

After this characteristic declaration, he proceeds to details, and from his keen, almost fierce descriptions, it will be easy to imagine what a race of scoundrels had been poured into Italy by the feeble Directory, He begins with the Company Flachat, which he styles a loose lot of rogues, without credit, money, or morality. Flachat and La Porte have little fortune and no credit; Pergallo and Payan are ruined houses. They are not merchants, but jobbers. They sell everything below the market price for their own profit. All the commissaries of war, one or two excepted, are rogues. "They sell everything," he repeats—"bark, grain, boots, mattresses, linen for the hospitals—but I stop—so many horrors make one blush to be a Frenchman!"

No doubt the Directory expected to be robbed by its servants; but they rob so impudently, that if he had a month to spare, there is not one he would not shoot. He would arrest them and bring them before a Council of War, but they buy the judges.

"This is a fair; everything is sold. An *employé,* accused of having levied a contribution of 18,000 *francs* on Salo, has been only condemned to two months in irons. How can you prove your charges? They are all in it." These were contractors: come to the administration. Thévenin is a robber, Auzou is a rogue, Sonolet is a rogue. "I only speak of the great robbers."

The military agents are all robbers; they try to seduce the general's secretaries in his very antechamber. They are, in his eyes, nearly all *émigrés*; nay, they correspond with the enemy, reveal the number of his troops, destroy his prestige. But tomorrow he must start to join the army; great delight among the sharpers, with whom a swift glance at them has made him acquainted! The complaint was general. Bonaparte hated unauthorized robbery. The rights of the conqueror he never scrupled to enforce; but indiscriminate, disorderly plundering was criminal in his eye. Some of the men, whose names he mentions, were afterwards acquitted; but that does not prove he was wrong, since one of the discoveries he made at Milan was that everything, even justice, was sold.

When he became master of despotic power, he put down the hordes of predatory animals, whom a lax rule at Paris had fostered into an evil activity. Certainly, however he may have plundered on a grand scale from one end of Europe to the other, he did not plunder to obtain wealth for himself. In one sense, he was a great robber; he was never a *fripon*. And well might he be enraged with his contractors and commissaries, when he saw his splendid little army suffering awful privations, because the Directory supplied him with a horde of scoundrels.

CHAPTER 6

Bonaparte and Alvinzi

Winter was approaching. The snow had already fallen in the Tyrol. The Austrian soldiery was again gathering there to tempt once more, under a new chief, the smiles of fortune. The Emperor, warring alike on the Rhine and in Italy, sent his third army against the young general, the echo of whose deeds had resounded through Europe, and who had revived on the plains of Lombardy and Venetia the military art.

Bonaparte, foreseeing that the crisis would be on the Adige, had declined to act on the suggestions of the Directory, which would have led him to Rome, or Naples, or Trieste, and confined himself to respectfully but firmly telling the Emperor of Austria that, unless he made peace, the French armies should capture and sack Trieste, and destroy the position of Austria on the Adriatic. He knew he could not carry out this threat at the moment when he made it; but he knew also that, providing a general keeps good guard, watches his foe, learns all his movements, and prepares for every emergency, he loses nothing by putting the boldest face on his affairs.

It is not our mode of making war. But hardy threats keep up the spirit of the French soldiery, who are almost invincible so long as they believe themselves to be so. Bonaparte never dissembled his own weakness to himself, but he never revealed it to his enemy. On the contrary, no general ever imposed upon his friends and his foes more than Bonaparte, and no general ever made such a brilliant use of the moral and immoral agents in war.

The French general, after his sojourn at Milan and his war with the rogues of the civil service, and after a swift journey to the Legations, arrived at Verona on the 23rd of October. Constantly demanding reinforcements from the Directory, to fill up the great gaps in his force occasioned by war and disease, aware that he would be compelled to fight once more for his conquests, he yet received few men, certainly not more than 6,000; and he bitterly complains of the generals who kept back the promised battalions.

To inspire the Italians with some confidence, and to supplement with native the deficiencies of foreign troops, he permitted Lombardy, Modena, and the Legations to raise more legions, and he called a portion of them to the banks of the Adige, to take part in the impending struggle. Early in October he had received from his secret and adroit agents the information that the Austrians had 14,000 men in the Tyrol, and 15,000 on the Piave. Looking at his own small army, he prepared for the worst; employed the smallest possible number of men to blockade Mantua effectually; armed small craft on the lakes, and placed all the strong or important places on his line of retreat as far as Alessandria in a state of defence.

Indeed, the efforts of the Emperor were as great as before. The success of the Archduke Charles on the Rhine had freed a part of the army placed in support; these and all disposable men were sent towards Italy. At the end of October, the Court of Vienna had assembled a well-equipped army of 28,000 men on the Piave, Isonzo, and Taglianento, and some 20,000 in the valley of the Upper Adige; and had given the command to Alvinzi, an officer who had seen the disasters that overtook Beaulieu and befell Wurmser, who knew the country and its capabilities, and who did not, like Beaulieu and Wurmser, encounter Bonaparte in ignorance of his mode of making war.

But Alvinzi was also old—upwards of sixty. He belonged essentially to the ancient school, and had won more laurels in the wars with the Turks than in war with more redoubtable foes. He was too slow, too methodical; he had too little audacity to contend with a man like Bonaparte. His army was more showy than substantial, and, its battalions of raw levies were not the troops which a general would have chosen to lead against the fiery and war-hardened veterans of the French Republic. It is remarkable that the chief of his staff, now about to front Bonaparte for the first time, was that very Weyrother, who, as chief of the staff of another army, was destined, eleven years later, to witness the utter failure of his combinations on the field of Austerlitz.

The larger wing of the Austrian army, 26,400 strong, was in Friuli, at the head of the Adriatic; the smaller, about 20,000 men, was north of Trent The former was under the immediate orders of Alvinzi, the latter under Davidowich. Alvinzi went to Botzen, the headquarters of the chief of his right wing, and there settled the plan of the campaign. As before, the army, which might have been easily united, was divided; and, undeterred by the severe lessons administered to his predecessors, Alvinzi resolved to operate upon two distinct and disconnected lines.

Davidowich was to march down the Adige to Verona; Alvinzi was to make for the same place across the Piave and Brenta. Arrived at Verona, the two wings were to unite, sweep the French across the Mincio, and, marching southwards, relieve Mantua and liberate Marshal Wurmser. The plan looked feasible, because the Austrians outnumbered the French, and knew well their own superiority in that respect. Something also was hoped for from the imprisoned Marshal, who, it was thought, might break out of Mantua, and help in the fight The two wings were, as much as possible, to regulate their marches; but Alvinzi showed too much timidity, and relied too much on the success of Davidowich.

To meet the storm, Bonaparte called up every man that could be spared. He had none too many. Out of 38,000 in Italy, and under his orders, he could not unite more than 24,000 at the utmost on the Adige; the rest were doing garrison duty in the towns of Italy and Piedmont, and blockading Mantua. In order to supply this great deficiency in numbers, he had to draw upon his genius, and the devotion of his lieutenants; the best of whom,

Massena, Augereau, Joubert, Gardanne, Lannes, Murat, were eager to display again those qualities which had led them from the Alps to the Tyrol. Bonaparte held his ground, ready to strike with either hand, and with both.

The enemy began his march from Friuli, on the 22nd October; and, on the 30th, the columns of his left were united behind the Piave. Massena, ever watchful, had kept, in obedience to his instructions, a sharp look out in his right front; and, on the 30th, his patrols were engaged with the advanced guard of the enemy, and he himself closely reconnoitred the Austrian force, drawn out to check any forward movement. On the 1st November, Alvinzi crossed the Piave; and Massena, feeling no longer secure in his advanced position, retired to Bassano, and thence, on the 4th, by the orders of Bonaparte, towards Vicenza. But the chief had called up Augereau to Montebello; and Massena, hearing this, halted his division a few miles from that city.

On the Adige, Vaubois was already engaged with the enemy. On the 30th, Valette had made a strong reconnaissance, and had found the enemy in force; and, on the 2nd November, Vaubois attacked the Austrian position in front of Lavis, drove in the advanced posts, and burnt a bridge over the Adige. On the 3rd, Davidowich, in turn, brought down superior forces, advanced with spirit, handled Vaubois very severely, and chased him all down the road to Trent, and through it, and far on towards Roveredo.

A third column of Austrians had also appeared. Loudon, operating on the right bank of the Adige, had fallen upon Gardanne's men, and had carried the position of Torbole. This was too precious to be lost, for it assured the retreat of the left upon Monte Baldo; and Gardanne, nothing loath, retook it by a night attack. Vaubois had taken up a position in the defile of Caliano, defended on each flank by a tower; and, on the 6th, Davidowich advanced from Trent with a great force, and fought all day for the possession of this defile.

The French stood that day; but, on the 7th, the Austrians fell on, with the dawn, carried the two towers by storm, and, pushing forward, compelled Vaubois to march with all speed down the Adige, to cross it in haste at Dolce, and hurry on to Rivoli. These combats were terrible, and bloody; and the French admit a loss of six pieces of cannon, and three thousand men in killed, wounded, and prisoners.

During this time, Bonaparte had joined Massena's army; and, bringing up the corps of Augereau, he directed an advance from Vicenza upon the Austrians, whom he hoped to defeat in detail. He found them, on the 6th, strongly posted behind the Brenta at Cittadella and Bassano. Massena attacked Liptay at Cittadella. The Brenta ran along the Austrian front, and the troops occupied an island in the stream, connected with the left bank by a bridge. Here the combat was long, hot, and bloody.

The river was fordable; it was crossed and recrossed more than once by both sides; the French vainly strove to carry the island, although Massena sustained the attack with the fire of eighteen guns, and the officers were prodigal of life and limb. At length Provera brought succour to Liptay, already a match for Massena, who then drew off his forces, and contented himself with demonstrations. Augereau had found Quasdanowich at Bassano in greater strength than he anticipated.

Driving the enemy from the village of Nove, Augereau pursued, until brought up in front of their main body. Here he waged a stout, but fruitless fight; for his reserve, commanded by Bon, had been arrested at the village of Nove by an Austrian Force, which had either concealed itself therein when the French rushed through, or had glided into Augereau's rear. Bon, therefore, had to carry the village before he could succour his chief; and the enemy defended himself so well that the force in front was nearly put to flight ere Bon came up and sustained them until dark. Both combats were well sustained, and the progress of Alvinzi had been checked.

Bonaparte found that he had no longer with him the men who defended the Monte Legino, and stormed the Bridge of Lodi; and he did not conceal his dissatisfaction. Vaubois had disappointed him. He relieved him of his separate command;

placed him under Massena; called up Joubert from Legnago, and sent him, at the top of his speed, with 2,000 men under Colonel Vignolles, to occupy the Corona without losing an instant It was of the utmost importance that the division of Vaubois should anticipate the enemy at the Corona, and hold it as long as possible. They must be master of the line, between the Adige and the Lake of Garda. Bonaparte also addressed this stinging rebuke to the vanquished of Caliano, dating it at Rivoli on the 7th, whither he had galloped after the combats on the Brenta.

> Soldiers!—I am not satisfied with you; you have not shown discipline, steadiness, or courage; no position has induced you to rally. You have been panic-struck; you have allowed yourselves to be driven from positions in which a handful of brave men would stop an army. Soldiers of the 39th and of the 85th! You are not French soldiers. General, Chief of the Staff, write on their banners—'*They no longer belong to the Army of Italy!*'

The defeat of Vaubois constrained Bonaparte to withdraw his troops from the Brenta; and on the 7th Massena and Augereau fell back to Vicenza. The Austrians followed, but slowly; Liptay, a ready officer, was prepared, but Provera had broken his bridge over the Brenta, and could not move until it was reconstructed. The French did not stay long in Vicenza, but retired towards Verona. Alvinzi therefore entered Vicenza on the 8th, and on the 9th encamped at Montebello. Hearing at this place of the victories of Davidowich on the Adige, he determined to hold his ground, and await Davidowich, whom he daily expected to see issuing from the valley. He chose a position at Villanova, and encamped there on the 11th.

Bonaparte had taken a rapid and searching survey of his position, and had adopted sage precautions, keeping a garrison in Legnago, a strong garrison in Verona, now of more moment to him than ever, because it enabled him to act on both banks of the river, and showing the greatest anxiety for the possession of Renco and the boats of its bridge. He still looked to his rear;

still called for men, money, guns, artillerymen; and endeavoured to impress on each officer that the security of Italy lay in the promptitude and completeness of his exertions. After the combats on the Brenta he ordered Massena to defend his left flank, to hold Monte Baldo, the Corona, Rivoli, and the narrow valley on the right bank of the Adige, giving him, as lieutenants, Vaubois, Joubert, Gardanne, Guyeu. Massena showed great activity, and covered his front with patrols on both banks.

To Augereau was confided the line of the Adige below Verona, and he fixed his headquarters at Ronco. Davidowich did not move, and Alvinzi lost precious hours in debates with his staff. On the 11th, Alvinzi, desirous of learning whether the French intended to hold Verona, sent the Prince of Hohenzollern towards it for the purpose of making Bonaparte show his hand. Hoping to cut them off, the latter passed through Verona, and, striking swiftly at the Austrian advance, drove it backward as far as the canal of Vago. The Austrian reserves saved the Prince, the night put an end to the combat, but Bonaparte was frustrated. Massena was called from Rivoli; each side prepared for a fiercer combat on the following day; and Bonaparte issued this spirited address to troops who, unaccustomed to defeat, required a stimulus.

Soldiers!—Mantua is without bread, without meat, without forage. Wurmser, the remnant of the army which you destroyed at Bassano, at Saint-Georges, at Governolo, is ready to fall into your hands. The liberty of Italy, the happiness of France, depend on your courage.

A heap of fugitives reinforced by the last reserves of the Emperor, venture to present themselves again before you. They will try to snatch from you the fruits of the victories of six months.

The generals will do their duty: they will all fall upon the enemy; sometimes they will lead you forward, sometimes they will feign a retreat, and they will neglect nothing that can add to the glory of your victory!

But as soon as the drum shall have beaten to battle, and

when you must march straight on the enemy with fixed bayonet, and in that solemn silence which is the guarantee of victory—Soldiers! remember then to be worthy of yourselves. I will only say two words to you, they will be sufficient for Frenchmen: Italy! Mantua! The peace of Europe, the happiness of your families, will be the result of your courage. Let us do once more what we have done so often, and Europe will not contest our right to the title of the bravest and most powerful nation in the world.

Alvinzi expected and had prepared for a combat on the 12th of November. He posted his army at Caldiero, on the heights below the post road from Verona to Vicenza.

"The heights of Caldiero," says Jomini, "are the spurs of the mountains of Sette Communi, which slope gradually to the Adige, and cross the post road from Verona to Vicenza. These heights—steep, covered with vineyards, planted on one side by the river, and on the other by the lofty mountains whence they jut forth—form one of the most remarkable of military positions."

Alvinzi held this strong position with one-third of his army, and kept the other two-thirds in reserve. He had abundance of field artillery, some guns of position, and considerable force of horsemen. Bonaparte, determined to remove him from his dangerous proximity to his right wing, caused Massena to march through Verona and attack the Austrian fight, while Augereau assailed their left. At the first onset fortune smiled upon the French; they carried one portion on the heights and the village of Colognola; but in the midst of his success, Alvinzi's brigadiers, detached from the main body, came unawares upon the French in front and flank; the wind blew fiercely from the north-east, and the rain as it fell froze in the faces of the soldiers.

Unable to stand against the vigorous blows of the enemy, and dispirited by the fury of the weather, Massena, who knew when a French soldier felt that he must soon run, withdrew his men by San Martino to Verona. Lannoy made a last effort to control the enemy, but he was speedily overthrown and taken prisoner.

On his side, Augereau had not been more fortunate. He also at first won some small advantages; but the Austrians were too well posted and too ably supported. Resisted in front, and turned on his right flank, Augereau, when he saw Massena in retreat, also fell back as best he could by San Michele to Verona.

In this day, so disastrous for the French, they admit that their loss was 900 killed and wounded, 800 prisoners and two guns.

How bitterly Bonaparte felt this defeat is shown by a paragraph in his despatch to the Directory on the 13th.

"The wounded," he writes, "are the *élite* of the army. All our superior officers, all our best generals are *hors de combat;* all those who arrive here are so stupid, the soldiers have no confidence in them. The army of Italy, reduced to a handful of men, is exhausted. The heroes of Lodi, Milesimo, Castiglione, Bassano, have died for their country, or are in hospital. All that remains to the corps is their reputation and pride. Joubert, Lannes, Lanusse, Victor, Murat, Chabot, Dupuy, Rampon, Chabran, Pijon, Saint Hilaire, Menard, are wounded. We are abandoned in the depth of Italy . . . . Those brave men who remain regard death as infallible amid such continual chances, and with forces so small. Perhaps, the hour of the brave Augereau, the intrepid Massena, of Berthier, of my own death, is about to sound . . . . We will make a last effort. If fortune smiles, we shall take Mantua, and with Mantua all Italy."

But heavy blows like this excited the genius of Bonaparte. He was far from being in the despairing frame of mind implied in this despatch. The array of losses was intended as a rebuke to the Directory for the abandonment of an army which had done so much to sustain the credit of the French arms in a land so often their grave. Bonaparte meditated at this moment that brilliant design, the happy execution of which showed him to be more redoubtable with 18,000 men than a merely scientific officer who has passed all the schools, and even seen war, with double the number.

Bonaparte placed his army in and in front of Verona, and remained quiet on the 13th and 14th. The generals of division inspected the armament of their corps, replenished their cartouche boxes, distributed food, and all the shoes they could lay hands on. Alvinzi remained idle at Caldiero, looking in vain for news of Davidowich, whose dispersed columns were skirmishing in front of Vaubois. Nevertheless, the position of that General became hourly more precarious. Up to the 13th, the corps of Davidowich was scattered over an immense extent of ground on both sides of the Adige, from Lugo to the head of the Garda Lake, On the 14th, Davidowich began to move. He pushed forward his columns on the Monte Baldo, to Brentino, the Corona, and Dolce on the left bank.

The French fell back all along their front, and in the afternoon of the 14th, Joubert received orders from Bonaparte to retire from the Corona, and take post at Rivoli, gathering up the troops on Monte Baldo and elsewhere, and leaving only 300 men in observation at the Corona. If attacked at Rivoli, Vaubois, the nominal commander, to whom the order was addressed, was to defend himself with the utmost obstinacy, in order to gain time. Gardanne and Guyeu were ordered to set out for Ronco by forced marches.

The troops that remained were ordered to light fires along the whole front, in order to impose upon the enemy. Ocskay, who commanded the right of the Austrians, had made but slow progress on the Monte Baldo; and Davidowich, taught precaution by so many reverses, was fain to halt and report his position to Alvinzi. At this time, although Ocskay had met with no great resistance, yet he was moving on, and the French were still on the Corona, Alvinzi ordered Davidowich to press on. In the night of the 14th, Joubert fell back on Rivoli, and the troops, ordered to reinforce Bonaparte in his meditated coup at Ronco, were on the march for that place.

Never had Bonaparte been in such a strait before. Here was Alvinzi, with far superior numbers, holding a most threatening position in his front. On his left flank another army, also far superior in number, was steadily, if slowly, forcing its way between the Adige and the Lake of Garda. His whole army, reduced by severe losses in the field, did not now amount to more than 13,000 men for the defence of Verona and operations against the enemy; and less than 8,000 to cover his left flank and the road on that side to Mantua.

If Bonaparte moved upon Davidowich, Alvinzi could cross the Adige and raise the blockade. If he resisted Alvinzi in front, Davidowich might overpower Joubert and Vaubois. It was under these disastrous circumstances that Bonaparte's genius for war suddenly shone forth with a brightness that bewildered his adversary, and astonished all Europe.

He resolved to cross the Adige at Verona, recross it at Ronco, alarm Alonizi for his communications, and beat him if he gave battle on the narrow causeways, where not numbers, but valour would be sure to prevail. It was dangerous; but so would be any resolve. The patient was suffering from a disease that might be mortal, and the remedy must be one that would kill or cure. Bonaparte counted, and justly, on the slowness and method of his adversary. Give him time, and he might win. Fight a campaign of combats instead of one of manoeuvres, and the small army must go to the wall, if only from loss of men.

Therefore, maintaining the profoundest secrecy, and even leading the officers to believe that the army was retreating towards Mantua, Bonaparte, on the night of the 14th and 15th, carried them in silence over the three bridges which span the Adige at Verona, and then suddenly turning to the left, filed down the right bank of the river to Ronco. He held fast, however, to Verona; it was his ark of safety; and to the Adige and its marshes, they were defences and supports quite as secure. His design, as stated by himself, was to seize Arcola, march on Villanova, carry off the enemy's park of artillery and his magazines, and attack him in flank and rear.

The battle of Arcola, a bloody fight of three days, is so remarkable, both in its incidents and issues, that it will be necessary to pay great attention to the description of the ground, which shall be rendered as clear as we can make it without the aid of plans.

Bonaparte had constructed his bridge at Ronco, about eleven miles from Verona, He had chosen this point, because it offered at once the greatest number of roads for assailing his enemy, and the best position of defence for himself. A short distance below Ronco, the river, Alpon, rising in the mountains of the Tyrol, pours like a torrent through the ravines; but, after passing the road from Verona to Vicenza, it creeps lazily through the plain past San Bonnifaccio and Arcola, and falls into the Adige, midway between Ronco and Albaredo. The country between the Alpon and the Adige is an extensive tract of marsh, here and there relieved by willow-trees, diversified by rice fields, and even containing some islands of firm land, in which are villages and farms.

Across this swamp ran several raised causeways connecting the villages together, and providing the country people with the means of communicating with each other. From Ronco, a road traversed the lower portion of the swamp, passed up the right bank of the Alpon to Arcola, and, crossing the river, thence along the left bank to San Bonnifaccio and the Vicenza road. On the left, from Ronco, another road, following a bold curve of the Adige, traversed the marshes by the village of Bionde to Porcil, whence it ascended to the firmer ground, and stretched away to Caldiero. From Bionde, also, there was a lower road, nearer to the Adige, and conducting to San Martino.

On the left bank of the Alpon, the road from Arcola passed through Albaredo, and continued down the left bank of the Adige to Legnago. It will be seen, therefore, that if Bonaparte could gain forty-eight hours upon Alvinzi, pass the bridge at Ronco, seize Porcil on the left and Arcola on the right; he could from Porcil fall upon the rear of the Austrian division in front of Caldiero, and from Arcola seize the village of San Bonnifaccio, and cut off Alvinzi at Villanova from Vicenza.

Alvinzi had also formed his project; but he was twenty-four

hours behind time. He proposed to pass the Adige at Zevio between Ronco and Verona, and he had established a small post
in front of Ronco, in order to protect his left. When he heard
that Bonaparte had secretly and swiftly passed through Verona,
marched rapidly down the Adige, crossed at Ronco, and thrown
forward columns to the right and left, he did not consider it a
serious attack, but a diversion; and, removing his parks of artillery and his baggage as far to the rear as Montebello, he still
dreamed of carrying out his design; but he was soon convinced
of his error.

Augereau crossed at Ronco early on the morning of the
15th, driving back the Croats, under Brigido, who retired by the
causeway as far as Arcola, and took post behind its narrow bridge
of wooden planks resting on piles of masonry, and protected on
either side by houses which the Croats had pierced for musketry. Augereau had rapidly followed them along the causeway;
but when he came to the bridge, his leading sections were shot
down, and his course was arrested by a front and flank fire from
the Croats. He, therefore, threw a battalion across the Alpon to
turn the village, while Lannes led two others upon the bridge
head. In vain the hero of Lodi showed the way; the soldiers
would not follow him; but, slipping behind the reverse slope of
the causeway, kept up a musketry fire upon their enemies.

This was a serious check for Bonaparte. He had counted
upon seizing Arcola, and he found himself arrested by a handful
of Croats. Two more battalions were directed against the bridge;
but the general who led them was mortally wounded; the soldiers ran back in disorder; when Augereau himself, seizing a
flag, cheered on his grenadiers to the charge. The fire was too
severe. Some of the old soldiers followed their leader; but the
rest, terror-stricken, slid down the bank, and vainly expended
their powder against the village.

Massena had crossed at Ronco, and directed his march along
the causeway leading to the left. By this time Alvinzi had become
convinced that Bonaparte meditated a real attack, and he had
sent a regiment of infantry through Porcil towards Ronco, and

strong supports to reinforce the Croats at Arcola. The causeways on the left were now full of troops; the Austrians were moving along both the roads leading from Porcil towards Ronco; their advanced guard drove back the French, took two pieces of cannon from them, and, pressing on round the curve of the Adige, nearly gained the bridge itself.

But Massena urged on his men, and one Austrian column, mistaking another for Frenchmen, opened fire upon it. Gardanne at the same moment, charging fiercely, retook the two guns, captured the village of Porcil, and also 800 prisoners, who, engaged on a lateral causeway, were cut off by the rapid march of the French along a shorter road.

Hearing of the ill success of Augereau at Arcola, Bonaparte sent General Guyeu with two battalions across the Adige at Albaredo, with instructions to move up the left bank of the Alpon upon Arcola. He hurried himself to the front of that village, the defenders of which had now been reinforced by a whole brigade. Seeing the necessity for a great effort, Bonaparte dismounted, and, seizing a flag, rushed forward, calling upon his soldiers to follow. But the men of Lodi were not before the bridge of Arcola. Bonaparte was only followed by his staff. Muiron was shot dead; Verdier, Vignolles, and Belliard were wounded at his side.

The soldiers fell into utter confusion, dropping behind the causeway, and pushing each other into the marsh. Bonaparte, who had been carried away by the crowd of fugitives, was himself hurled into the mud, and was in danger of being engulphed together with his brother Louis, when Marmont and two subalterns dragged him out by main force. Belliard, although wounded, collected a handful of grenadiers, and, turning upon the enemy, who had followed closely, drove them back towards the bridge, thus giving Bonaparte time to complete his escape. At the same time the defenders of Arcola attacked the battalion sent by Augereau to the left bank of the Alpon, and compelled them to recross it.

When Bonaparte had withdrawn his columns both from the

Porcil and Arcola causeways back to Ronco, and the Austrians were reposing in the belief that they had won the day, Guyeu, coming up from Albaredo, fell suddenly upon their troops in Arcola, and, after a short resistance, drove them out, and forced them back as far as San Bonnifaccio. And here occurred one of those strange incidents which sometimes frustrate the best arranged plans in war.

Guyeu finding himself alone, and having received no orders from his chief, Massena—to whose division he was attached—instead of holding Arcola on his own responsibility, gave up what he had so hardly won, and fell back upon Albaredo. Thus, although Guyeu had actually accomplished what Augereau and Bonaparte had vainly essayed, the French army at the close of the 15th, found itself exactly in the same position in which it was at daybreak. The Austrians on either side, now alive to the serious character of Bonaparte's design, had occupied all the causeways and sent two battalions to Albaredo; and Alvinzi hoped by a concentric movement upon Ronco from Porcil and Arcola to defeat his opponent. Note, the force of the Austrians, on the night of the 15th, was full 20,000 men, while that of their opponents did not reach half the number. In this situation of things terminated the first day of the battle of Arcola.

On the 16th, at daybreak, Bonaparte once more renewed the combat, fighting with both bands—Massena striking out with the left, and Augereau with the right. Massena followed the causeways that led towards Porcil, having in front of him his old enemy, Provera. For some time the leaders of the two opposing columns kept up a smart skirmish; the Austrians being sustained by two pieces firing grape. Gardanne, always alive to an advantage, led some companies of grenadiers along a tongue of reedy marsh, that stretched out in a line parallel to the Austrian advance, and fired into their right flank.

A protracted combat of this kind was not suited to the genius of that French general; and, placing his hat upon his sword, he mounted on the causeway and charged the Austrians. Twice, volleys of grape compelled the French to throw themselves flat on the ground; but at length their courage rose equally to that of their general; they dashed forward with their old impetuosity. The brigades in the rear caught the same spirit, and, pressing on with the bayonet, drove the Austrians back along the causeway, or into the marshes through the village of Porcil, and up the slopes towards Albaredo. The fruit of the fighting on the left was the possession of five pieces of cannon and the field of battle.

Once more Augereau took his way along the right bank of the Alpon, towards the bridge of Arcola, but he was not happier on the 16th than he had been on the 15th. His first attack was repelled. In his second, supported by two guns, he obtained a greater success, and for a moment captured two pieces belonging to the enemy; but Alvinzi had now brought the greater part of his force in rear on the Alpon, and had garnished the brink of that river below Arcola with several battalions. The fire of these men across the river arrested Augereau in his career, and forced him to fly, leaving the captured cannon behind. Alvinzi now further, reinforced the whole of his position on the left bank of the Alpon, and succeeded in arresting all further attacks upon Arcola by the steadiness and accuracy of their fire.

Bonaparte, giving up all attempts to carry the Bridge of Arcola, endeavoured to throw a column across the Adige, at a point where it receives the waters of the Alpon. His first attempt was made in boats; but Miloradowich, an officer destined at a future day to come again in contact with Bonaparte, kept so good a watch at this point that he frustrated the attempt midway. Chasseloup and Vial, men good at need, were now directed to throw a bridge across the Alpon above its *embouchure* in vain.

Next, dismounted dragoons endeavoured to make a bridge with fascines, but the current carried them away. Vial now forded the river to show the way, and several officers followed him, yet the troops would not budge, and Vial and his brother officers, much mortified, were compelled to return. So ended the day. Bonaparte still occupied the angle formed by the Adige and the Alpon, with one battalion. Massena encamped on the causeway towards Porcil; and the rest of the troops were again withdrawn behind the Adige at Ronco.

Although the Austrians had been fortunate in repelling the assaults of their adversaries, yet they had suffered great losses, and Alvinzi, feeling the necessity of strengthening his position on the Alpon, recalled the greater part of the troops from Porcil and Caldiero. Bonaparte on his side, learning that Joubert still remained untouched at Rivoli, determined to adopt new tactics. He had a battalion and five hundred horsemen at Legnago, and on the night of the 16th, he ordered these to march up the left bank of the Adige, clearing the road of Austrian outposts, and alarming their left flank. He also determined to throw a bridge over the Alpon, and carry his army to the left bank. Chasseloup cleverly threw his bridge during the night.

On the 17th, the third day of the battle, once more the French columns marched forward on the causeways, to the right and to the left; again Provera was driven from Porcil, and the Austrian light troops hurried back to Arcola. Over the bridge which he had constructed in the night, unknown to the enemy, Bonaparte sent one battalion at the moment when he caught sight of the troops coming from Legnago. The battalion on the left of the Alpon, at first successful, was driven back towards the bridge, but, supported by Augereau, they overpowered the enemy, captured Albaredo, two horse artillery guns, and joined the horse and foot coming from Legnago; these troops united were to march upon Arcola. At this moment the Austrians on the right of the Alpon drove back the French towards Ronco, and the battalions on the left bank, taking fright, fled back across the bridge. The French right was now pressed back as far as the bridge of Ronco, and followed by the exulting foe.

Bonaparte had drawn a battalion from Verona, and had posted it in a clump of willows, on the right of the causeway leading from Ronco to Arcola. When he saw the troops of Augereau flying towards Ronco, he sent an express to Massena at Porcil, with urgent orders for that general to return instantly to Ronco.

The consequences of this movement was that the Austrians were attacked in rear by Massena, and on the left flank by the troops darting from the ambuscade, They were, therefore, completely cut off, destroyed, or taken prisoners, and the handful who escaped towards Arcola were followed at speed by Gardanne.

The Austrians were now in line behind the Alpon, their left resting on a marsh opposite Bonaparte's bridge, and their right upon Arcola, Augereau recrossed the Alpon; and the battle recommenced with fury on the right of the French. But as Augereau made little progress, and, as it was of the last importance that Bonaparte should carry his point, his fertile brain conceived a stratagem which had the happiest results. He ordered Lieutenant Hercule, an officer of his Corps of Guides, to pass the Adige with twenty-five resolute men, and all the trumpets he could scrape together. Hercule obeyed his chief, crossed the river, turned the marsh which supported the Austrian left, and galloped into their rear, sounding the charge with all his trumpets. The stratagem was most successful. The Austrian right, believing that they were turned by a column of cavalry, rapidly retired from their position. Augereau advanced swiftly upon Arcola and Gardanne, and made a new attempt upon the bridge on the right bank.

Fortune had always favoured the French on their extreme left, Provera, who had remained near Porcil, was directed to create a diversion, by following the causeway towards Ronco. Massena instantly despatched a body of troops to meet this new attack, Provera had nearly enveloped his foe, by moving on several causeways, when Lieutenant Chatelain, with twenty horsemen ranged four abreast, charged one of the enemy's columns on the causeway, and captured their artillery. The infantry pressing on, Provera was driven back to Caldiero, and retired at once to Villanova. Released from all fear on his left, Massena marched up the right bank of the Alpon, to support the attack upon Arcola.

Alvinzi's position was now no longer tenable; and as he retired, Augereau and Massena entered Arcola from different sides. Alvinzi retired towards San Bonnifaccio; and the French extended in line of battle round Arcola. In the night the Austrians attempted to surprise the sleeping troops, and had some success, but were eventually repulsed. The next day, the Austrian chief, hearing nothing from Davidowich, withdrew his army to Montebello.

The loss of the Austrians during these three days of constant fighting, is estimated at 535 killed, 1,535 wounded, and 4,141 prisoners, and 11 guns. The French were more severely treated; the general officers, Bon, Verdier, Lannes, Verne, Robert, Gardanne, Belliard, Vignolles, were wounded. In the two divisions, Massena, Augereau, Guyeu, alone escaped with whole skins. The gross loss amounted to 4,500 men, of whom 1,000 were killed, 2,300 wounded, and 1,200 taken prisoners.

During the battles at Arcola, Joubert, who commanded the French, left between the Adige and the Lake of Garda, was exposed to a series of fierce onsets from Davidowich, who, urged on by Alvinzi, endeavoured to overthrow the French left, and join his chief. But he did not move until the 17th, and it was then too late. His columns came over the Monte Baldo, and down the roads on the right and left banks of the Adige. A series of combats, characterised by great vicissitudes on both sides, but which it would be profitless to explain in detail, were carried on during the whole day.

Some of the French troops showed great courage; and Joubert, as usual, was foremost in the attack, and present at every point where there was danger. But others of the French troops, fighting in the ravines and the hills, in the face of double their number of foes, showed little courage in attack, and no tenacity when assailed. The Austrians came trooping in on all sides, and Joubert was compelled to retire his men as best he could, on the road to Peschiera.

Davidowich had delayed his advance too long, and when he achieved the, success which we have indicated, he was suddenly compelled to give ground by the troops of Massena, whom Bonaparte had ordered from the pursuit of Alvinzi against his lieutenant. Joubert once more advanced. Guillaume sent some troops across the lake of Garda into the right rear of the enemy. Augereau, passing through the mountains on the left bank of the

Adige, threatened Wukassowich. Alvinzi, being informed of the movement of Bonaparte upon the Upper Adige, returned on the 22nd of November to his old position at Arcola and Caldiero. But the success of Bonaparte against Davidowich was too decisive; and, fearing to be anticipated at Bassano by the corps of Augereau, which might have moved down the valley of the Brenta, Alvinzi once more withdrew and took post behind that river, while Davidowich, on his side, fell back to Roveredo.

Wurmser had peacefully remained blockaded in Mantua, looking for the expected army of relief throughout the brief campaign. It had been calculated that Alvinzi would reach Mantua about the 23rd, and Wurmser had undertaken to make a sortie on that day. This arrangement proved fortunate for the French; they were able to reinforce the blockading division; and when Wurmser made a powerful and combined attack upon the French position in the Faubourg of St. George, he was forced back into the place, after a hard day's fighting, with a loss of two guns and 800 men. Thus, the fourth campaign of the Austrians against Bonaparte had failed, and Marshal Wurmser was shut up more closely than ever in his Mantuan prison.

The French army had now another interval of repose in their old quarters between Mantua and the valley of the Upper Adige. Bonaparte had his headquarters at Milan part of the time, and part of the time at Verona. From these two places he kept up an incessant surveillance upon the organization and disposition of the army; upon the politics of the conquered country; upon the courts of Florence, Some, and Turin; upon the Venetians; and upon the "*fripons.*"

At the end of November he took measures to fill his military chest He caused the taxes imposed by the Republic, and the remains of the contribution to be more rapidly collected and paid. He laid hands upon all Austrian property, and sold it. The value of abbeys and benefices was realized, and the silver in the churches seized and sold. The Lombard Chamber of Commerce was to lend 1,200,000 *livres*, and a tax was levied upon absentees. Lombardy was to lend him 8,000,000, and, if this did not prove sufficient, the amount was to be raised to the level of his requirements.

Supported by General Clarke, who had reached his head-quarters from Paris, Bonaparte insisted anew upon having prompt reinforcements. He showed that, unless he were reinforced, the Republic would lose the money the Pope had promised to pay, and would also not take Mantua.

"Lombardy," wrote Clarke, "is exhausted, and we must have the money, not only for the army of Italy, but for the army of the Rhine."

He was, therefore, opposed to an armistice with the Emperor, which would defer the capture of Mantua indefinitely, and enable the Pope still to keep his gold.

"Send me 30,000 men," said Bonaparte, "and I will march to Vienna, or at least maintain the war in the states of the Emperor, live at his expense, ruin his subjects, and carry war and insurrection into Hungary." But the Directory answered these appeals by promises, and only sent a few thousand men, after long delays. In the meantime the troops at Mantua captured a spy sent from the Emperor to Wurmser, and, from the contents of his despatches, Bonaparte learned two important facts—the deplorable condition of the garrison, and the project of the enemy to renew the war in January, 1797.

The internal state of Italy was not altogether satisfactory. Rusca, in Modena, was forced to combat insurrection, applying the Bonapartist formula—fire, lead, and steel. Rusca was ordered to seize twenty hostages, and send them to Milan; to burn down the house of the confessor of the Duke of Modena, the author of the rebellion, erect where it stood a pyramid, and inscribe upon it these words—*The punishment of a furious priest, who, abusing his ministry, preached revolt and assassination.* Rusca was to assemble the magistrates and clergy, and menace them with a similar chastisement.

Writing to the Directory, on the 28th December, 1796, Bonaparte said—

There are three parties in Lombardy: first, those who are led by the French; second, those who wish for liberty, and even impatiently manifest their desires; thirdly, the friends of the Austrians and enemies of the French. I sustain and encourage the first, control the second, and repress the third.

Across the Po there were also three parties, and here, too, Bonaparte sustained and encouraged the middle party, who desired a constitution and independence, flattering them with a national army, and continually talking of the future great Italian power of which they were the nucleus.

At Milan he was engaged in a war *à l'outrance* with the cheats and rogues in the civil service. His old cry, "Everything is sold," finds a place in his despatches. "The keepers of the magazines forge false orders, and go halves with the commissaries. The *employés* of the French army keep the principal actresses in Italy; luxury, depravity, *malversation*, are at the highest pitch."

The laws were too weak in the eyes of one who loved sharp processes; and he wanted a kind of travelling commission with power, for two or three days at a time, to shoot any administrator whatever. Not that he was lax himself in the pursuit of knaves. "I cause some to be arrested daily; I overlook their papers and strong boxes, but I am seconded by nobody." He was naturally disgusted that the army should often want bread in a land of abundance.

Elsewhere than in Italy the French were not fortunate. They had been driven back to the Rhine, and had remained idle before Mayence. The expedition to Ireland and troubles in the south of France detained for a long time a portion of the troops ordered by the Directory to Italy; but a considerable number, detached from the Rhine, marched to join Bonaparte towards the beginning of 1797. In order to protect himself from the efforts which an enemy coming from the Valteline might make on his rear, he caused Baraguay d'Hilliers to seize the castle of Bergamo. Such was the position of affairs at the end of 1796.

CHAPTER 7

Alvinzi and Bonaparte in 1797

In the first days of January, 1797, the Austrian army occupied a long line, stretching from Padua to the Voralberg. Provera was at Padua, Quasdanowich at Bassano, with a flanking corps in the Val Sugana. Wukassawich was at Ala on the Adige, Weidenfield at Roveredo, Ocskay on the Monte Baldo, and on his right there was a flanking column. On the French side Joubert faced the Austrians in the valley of the Adige; Massena guarded that river from a point below Rivoli to Verona; Augereau had the care of the line on the right, with a strong post at Legnago, and he patrolled as far as Montebello and Vicenza. They had remained in these positions for more than two months, and both armies, but the Austrian especially, had made great exertions to prepare for the struggle.

Alvinzi determined to attack in three columns. On the left, Provera, with 9,000 men and ten guns, was to march from Padua upon Legnago, capture that place, if possible; if not, throw a bridge over the Adige, hasten towards Mantua, and act in concert with the garrison. A force of 6,240 men under Bajalich was to move on Verona; and smaller corps were to occupy the Val Sugana, and manoeuvre on the Lakes Garda and Iseo. The main army, 28,000 strong, commanded by Alvinzi, in person, was to carry the positions between the Lake of Garda and the Adige, and debouch upon Verona by Rivoli. The main body was itself subdivided into six columns, following the course of the practicable roads through the mountains.

This complicated plan, supposed to be the work of Weyrother, is cited by military men as a proof of the deplorable consequences that flow from the employment of science, when science is not governed by a just appreciation of circumstances. It was circumstances that prevented Bonaparte from having any plan beyond the simple and comprehensive one of holding his troops well in hand in their central position, ready to make head in any direction, to strengthen either side at pleasure, or unite his army in front of the most serious attack.

Bonaparte was at Bologna, signing a treaty with the Grand Duke of Tuscany, when Provera moved from Padua on the 7th of January, and Bajalich from Bassano on the 10th. Augereau lined the Adige with his division, posting the bulk at Ronco. At this time Bajalich had reached Caldiero, and Bonaparte had come up to Roverbella, bringing with him Lannes and 2,000 men. As he entered Verona, he learnt that Massena had been attacked by Bajalich, at St. Michel, in front of Verona, that the French were victorious, and that 500 prisoners and two guns had been taken.

Provera had arrived before the Adige, and still lingered on the left bank on the 12th. Alvinzi had also moved. But now the vice of his scheme was demonstrated. His brigadiers, tied down by instructions, waited for each other. The Monte Baldo separated the right from the centre; the Monte Magnone cut off the centre from the left; and the Adige interposed between the corps on its left bank, and both centre and wings. The troops on the mountains were without guns and cavalry, which marched in the valley along the brink of the Adige. The snow was on the mountains; the roads were rotten; the days were short Nevertheless, the columns of the enemy came steadily, if slowly, down the valley of the Adige, and climbed and descended its rough mountainsides.

On the 12th, when Bonaparte had just reached Verona, while Bajalich was hanging back on the Vicenza road, and Provera lingering uncertain in front of Legnago, Joubert on the Corona found enemies arise on all sides. Lusignan, with 4,000 men, had climbed the Monte Baldo on his left. Liptay, with 12,000, was in his front, Quasdanowich, with 8,000, was coming down from Rivalta on his right, and Wukassowich, with 4,000, on the left bank of the Adige, had reached Dolce. Joubert, therefore, fell back to Rivoli, where all the paths of the mountains meet, except one which, descending the Monte Baldo, passes to the west of Rivoli. Here Joubert halted; but, in the face of such strong columns as those that touched him on all sides, and having lost a battalion on the Monte Baldo, he was undecided whether to stand or retire.

By this time Bonaparte had ascertained to his own satisfaction that the great attack was by Rivoli, and he instantly determined to sustain Joubert He went at once to Rivoli; ordered thither a portion of Massena's corps; called up Victor from Castellaro in the Mantua country to Villafranca; Rey from Salo to Rivoli, and a detachment from Augereau. He placed a strong garrison in Verona, and urged Augereau to be on the alert, and attack if he thought fit

The Austrians had now united three of their columns in front of Rivoli, having Caprino on their right, and the chapel of San Marco, on the ridge of Magnone, on their left. But Lusignan was still on the further slope of the Monte Baldo, Quasdanowich, in the valley of the Adige, on one side of the river, and Wukassowich on the other. Bonaparte arrived at midnight. The moon shone brightly over the mountains, and the fires of the bivouacs glowed cheerfully in the chill night.

Well acquainted with the ground, Bonaparte could learn the exact facts from Joubert, and hence decide upon the best line of action. Alvinzi had formed his plan; but Bonaparte determined to be first, and to attack rather than wait to be assailed; for if the Austrians could have taken the position occupied by Joubert from Zoane to Osteria, they would have been able to unite their whole forces in front of Rivoli on a field where all arms could be used with effect

Wherefore, disregarding Lusignan, and not waiting for Massena and Rey, the French chief put his troops in motion before daylight. On the right, Joubert and Vial surprised the chapel of San Marco, and, after a severe combat, entrenched themselves there, but could not gain the heights above. In the centre, the Austrians were violently assailed and driven backward upon San Giovanni and Gambarone; on the left, the French carried the heights of Trombalora, and were reinforced from Rivoli along their whole line.

The Austrian generals were not willing to give up the fruit of so much labour and enterprise. They assembled their battalions and made counter attacks, especially on San Marco—a point of great importance. The French were rudely struck. Quasdanowich had arrived at Incanale, below the defile leading into the rear of the French, and was only held in check by a weak force posted at Osteria. Bonaparte, therefore, resolved to press on, directing the troops on his left upon San Giovanni; but as Liptay made a forward movement at the same time, and came on in strength and great resolution, a fierce combat ensued. The Austrians routed two brigades; they were stopped a moment by Berthier at the head of a third; then Berthier assailed in front and flank, yielded, and the Austrians took two guns. Rallied by their officers, the defeated brigades once more faced about, and, rushing headlong upon the enemy, recaptured the cannon.

At this crisis in the fight, when Bonaparte had engaged all his reserves, and when the battle seemed going against him, Massena, who had marched all night from Verona, where he had fought the day before, arrived on the field, and instantly threw himself into the contest The troops of the left wing, inspired by the spectacle of fresh soldiers, emulated them, and the enemy was expelled from the position.

But new dangers had arisen. The battle was far from being won. Vial had been driven from San Marco, and chased into the little village of Mutole in the valley. Wukassowich had marched down the left bank of the Adige nearly as far as Ceradino, and had planted a battery in a position whence he could send his shot across the river against the small garrison which kept the head of the defile of Incanale at Osteria. Thus aided, Quasdanowich on his side pressed up the defile, and drove its defenders before him. This was the turning point of the day. The genius of Bonaparte, the intrepidity of Berthier, the shining bravery of Joubert, at this crisis, saved the army.

Nevertheless, Quasdanowich gained ground. He carried the entrenchment at the head of the defile, and the head of his column began to form in its front But Joubert, placing his division on their flank, said leading his grenadiers like one of their own sergeants, musket in hand—and Berthier bringing up a demi-brigade in their front—and Leclerc charging with some horse, they impelled the head of the column back into the narrow defile, already choked up with guns and horsemen; and smiting them with musketry and cannon shot, threw them into disorder, which was augmented by the chance explosion of some ammunition wagons. Quasdanowich was thus provided for.

Yet the enemy were not defeated. The Austrians at San Marco had hastened down to aid Quasdanowich, and had seized Mutole. Joubert, therefore, having hurled his enemy down the defile of Incanale, turned to meet the new foe, who had earlier in the fight dispossessed him of San Marco. At this moment, Massena, moving from the left, came also upon the enemy, and thus attacked in front and flank, he fell into disorder, and retired as far as San Giovanni.

Lusignan had now come down the Monte Baldo as far as Affi in the rear of the French army; and, moving to his left, crossed the intervening hills, drove in the outposts on that side, and took a position on the Monte Pipolo, in rear of Rivoli, and across the French line of communications with Verona. This had not been unlooked for, and Bonaparte knew that he was safe, because General Rey was at that time coming up to Rivoli from Castelnuovo.

No sooner had Lusignan arrived, than Massena sent against him two battalions and four guns, and soon after Rey fell upon his flank and rear. Thus surrounded, the greater part of his force surrendered, and the rest fled laterally towards the Lake of Garda, where they were nearly all gathered up by the French flankers covering the Peschiera road. But Lusignan himself hid in an old castle, and escaped the next day.

Bonaparte was satisfied with the day, but Alvinzi was not yet beaten. Ranged behind a torrent from Caprino to San Martino, and still holding the chapel of San Marco and the ridge of Magnone, his hope revived on hearing the fire of Lusignan's troops in the enemy's rear at Rivoli. But Bonaparte feared him no longer. Recalled by intelligence that Provera had passed the Adige near Legnago, he had carried off in the night four demi-brigades, and had sent Massena with three regiments of cavalry to Roverbella. In their absence, Joubert, on the morning of the 15th, renewed the attack. Vial retook the chapel of San Marco after a series of sanguinary onsets, during which he was thrice repulsed,

Then, sending Vial along the crest to anticipate the Austrians at the Corona, he assailed them in front with the brigades of Baraguay d'Hilliers, and turned their right with a column under Murat The combination was successful, and the Austrians were driven far up the valley. The troops on the left bank of the Adige, seeing the fate of their comrades, faced about and made their way to the rear. The fruit of the combats at Rivoli was upwards of 6,000 prisoners and six guns.

During these sanguinary and obstinate combats, so honourably to the soldiers on both sides, but so little creditable to the Austrian school of war, Provera had begun to make his diversion on the side of Mantua. He selected Anghiari, near Legnago, as his point of passage. The only French troops at hand to dispute the right bank with him was a small body under General Guyeu, for the demonstrations of Bajalich about Verona detained a force in that quarter. Making two feints at different points, Provera suddenly threw his bridge across at Anghiari.

Guyeu, with a weak force, could not prevent him, and he carried his men safely over on the 13th, and interposed between Guyeu and Augereau who was at Legnago. But his business was not to fight combats on the Adige; it, was his object to reach Mantua, and, if possible, force a road through the blockading divisions. He therefore made the best of his way onward. Augereau, however, followed by parallel roads, and overtaking his rear guard, entangled in some rice grounds, he overthrew it, and took many prisoners.

Bonaparte had hastened from Rivoli on the night of the 14th, in order to succour Mantua. He outstripped the troops of Massena, who, although they had fought at Rivoli on the 14th, yet reached Roverbella on the 15th, a march of five-and-twenty miles. On that day, Provera's advanced guard was before the Faubourg of St George, but failed to surprise it Then he tried the post of La Favorite; his attempt was equally unsuccessful Victor had arrived from Villafranca with a reinforcement; and Serurier, who commanded the blockade, awoke to the danger, occupied the roads on his left, and pushed between La Favorite and Mantua. Provera was therefore frustrated.

On the 16th, Provera renewed his attack upon La Favorite; and Wurmser made a sortie. Again they were too late. Bonaparte had so strongly reinforced the blockading corps, bringing down Massena, Augereau, Victor, Guyeu, that he was able not only to drive Wurmser back into the fortress, but to surround Provera and the whole of his troops. He was assailed, driven from side to side, overthrown, and compelled at length to lay down his arms; but obtained from the French the honours of war. The only Austrian success during the day was won by the garrison, who for a short time held the village of San Antonio.

Practically this was the end of the campaign against Alvinzi. The exploit at La Favorite, say the French, gave them 7,000 prisoners, and 22 guns. In three days they had destroyed an army of 40,000, and had taken 20,000 prisoners, and 45 guns. It was on this occasion that Bonaparte, between whom and Massena, at this period, no love was lost, was constrained to give that general the poetic title of the *enfant chéri de la victoire*.

After this immense success, Bonaparte sent Joubert on the traces of Alvinzi, and Augereau and Massena to the Brenta. The Austrian rear-guards gallantly fought for every inch of ground; but their enemies were too strong and too elated; and early in February Joubert was on the Avisio at Lavis, and Massena and

Augereau had driven the enemy across the Piave. The French then took positions between Trent and Bassano, to await the capitulation of Mantua. Wurmser did not delay long. His means of subsistence were exhausted. On the 2nd February he signed the act of capitulation; and on the 3rd, French troops occupied the citadel.

The garrison marched out with the honours of war, then laid down their arms, and were to be prisoners until regularly exchanged, except Marshal Wurmser and the whole of his staff. The Marshal also stipulated for six guns, and carried his point, and horses for himself and his officers. Bonaparte was glad to obtain the fortress of Mantua on such terms. He found therein all the siege guns, 179 in number, abandoned when Wurmser made his first campaign; and, in addition to these, 328 guns and 60 colours. Augereau was intrusted with the pleasant task of carrying these to Paris. On the 3rd February, Bonaparte, in rendering to the Directory an account of his successes, does honour to the veteran who had fallen into his hands:—

"I am anxious," he says, "to show French generosity towards Marshal Wurmser, a general seventy years of age, towards whom fortune has been, in this campaign, very cruel; but who has, nevertheless, not ceased to show a courage and constancy of which history will keep account. Surrounded on all sides at the battle of Bassano, losing at one blow a part of the Tyrol, and his army, he dared to hope that he might fly for refuge in Mantua, which is four or five days' journey distant. He passed the Adige, overthrew one of our outposts at Cerea, crossed the Molinella, and arrived in Mantua. Shut up in this city, he made two or three sorties. All were unfortunate, and he led them all. But, besides the considerable obstacles presented by our lines of circumvallation, bristling with field pieces, which he was obliged to surmount, he could only act with soldiers who were discouraged by so many defeats, and weakened by the pestilential diseases of Mantua. The majority of men, who are always ready to calumniate the unfortunate, will not fail to persecute Wurmser."

Before Mantua surrendered, Bonaparte, who had long chafed at the insolence of the Court of Rome, resolved to carry the war into the States of the Church, and bring the Pope to terms. As early as the 20th of January, Victor was ordered to lead a moveable column across the Po. Two days afterwards, Bonaparte warned Cardinal Mattel, a prelate whom he always treated with civility, that the comedy they were playing at Rome was near its *denoûment*. Whatever might happen, he said, Mattel was to assure the Pope that he might rest safely at Rome. "First Minister of Religion, he will find in this title a protection for himself and the Church." The people of Rome would find in the French army friends "who congratulate themselves upon victory, only to ameliorate the lot of the people, and free Italy from the domination of strangers." Above all things, Bonaparte's particular care should be not to suffer any change in "the religion of our fathers."

A week afterwards, Victor was informed that Lannes would lead his advanced guard; Lannes,. who had shown as much promptitude and relentlessness at Binasco and Arquata as he had at Lodi and Arcola. Victor and Lannes crossed the Po; and, by the 1st of February, were in the heart of the Roman States. Bonaparte, who had gone to Bologna, sent before his columns one of those truculent proclamations which are one of the characteristics of his war in Italy:—

The French army enters the territory of the Pope: it will be true to the maxims it professes—will protect religion and the people.
The French soldier carries in one hand the bayonet, sure guarantee of victory; with the other, he offers to the different towns and villages, peace, protection, and safety. Woe to those who, wantonly seduced by profound hypocrites and wicked men, shall draw down on their homes the horrors of war, and the vengeance of an army which has, in six months, made prisoners of 100,000 men of the

best troops in Europe, taken 400 cannons, 110 colours, and destroyed five armies! Therefore—

1. Every village or town which, on the approach of the French army, shall sound the tocsin, shall be instantly burned, and the municipal authorities shot there and then.

2. Any commune within whose limits a Frenchman shall be assassinated, shall be instantly declared in a state of war; a moveable column shall be employed therein, hostages shall be taken, and an extraordinary contribution shall be levied.

3. All the priests, monks, ministers of religion, whatever they may be called, shall be protected, and maintained in their actual state,—if they behave according to the principles of the Gospel. If they are the first to transgress them, they shall be under military law, and be treated as severely as any others.

Bonaparte's political views, or at least those he thought fit to send to Paris, at this period, are interesting. He proposed to unite Modena, Parma, and the Romagna, and give them a republican government. He thought Rome might be given to Spain, if Spain would guarantee the new republic. In that case, if they were obliged to go that length to hasten a peace of which they stood in need, the French might restore the Milanese and the Mantuan to the Emperor, and give him also the Duchy of Parma. The Emperor, he reasoned, would lose nothing; Spain would gain a great deal; France would gain more: "we should have in Italy a natural ally, which would become powerful, and with whom we could correspond by Massa-Carrara and the Adriatic." Such were Bonaparte's views in February 1797. Subsequent events changed them vastly.

The French soon overcame the weak resistance offered by the Papal troops. On the march, Faenza, bigotedly devoted to Rome, sounded the alarm, closed its gates, and fired on Victor. Of course it was soon reduced to silence. Greatly to his credit,

Bonaparte did not execute the threats contained in his proclamation. How could he punish a whole town for the crime of a few priests. Nevertheless, his soldiers pillaged the people, the battalions of the Lombard and Polish legions, recently formed, emulating their French liberators; and Bonaparte severely rebuked them in an order of the day, and threatened them with death. Victor was informed that he was at the head of a *corps d'armée,* and not a horde of plunderers; and he was brusquely told to establish order and maintain a severe discipline.

Marching by Imola, Faenza, Forli, Rimini, Pesaro, Sinigaglia, to Ancona, he drove the Papal soldiery before him, and thus mastered in a few days the Romagna, the Duchy of Urbino, and the March of Ancona. At Loretto he nearly laid hands on all the treasure. What the Papal troops had left behind he seized, and packed off to the Directory, the wooden image of Our Lady of Loretto, and all the relics, to enrich the Museum of the Republic Bonaparte was too politic to interfere with religion more than was necessary; and while he privately asserted to the Directory, that Rome, deprived of Bologna, Ferrara, and the Romagna, and the thirty millions he was about to extort, could no longer exist—that the old machine, left to itself, would break down; in his letter to the Pope, after the peace of Tolentino, Bonaparte said that his Holiness would find the French Republic one of his best friends; and to enforce his words he sent Marmont to Rome to express to the Pope the esteem, the perfect veneration, he had for his person.

The treaty of Tolentino was signed on the 19th of February. The Pope retired from the coalition, and disbanded his newly raised army. He gave up absolutely his pretended rights to the city and territory of Avignon, and the Comtat Venaissin and its dependencies. He ceded the legations of Bologna, Ferrara, and the Romagna to the French, and gave up to them Ancona, its towns and territories, until a general peace was concluded. He undertook to pay 15,000,000 *livres tournois,* due from the old contribution, and 15,000,000 *livres tournois* in addition, either in money, diamonds, or other values; 10,000,000 in March, and the rest in April. France ceded to the Pope the French religious foundations in Rome and Loretto, and the Pope gave up to France all that belonged to him in the Legations. Thus the general obtained that money from the Pope for which he hungered and thirsted a short time before.

As he marched along, Bonaparte, looking to the future, organized local governments; and on quitting the Legations, he placed the new acquisitions of the Republic under the orders of Sahuguet He did not forget the cupidity of Paris.

"The commission of *savants*," he wrote from Tolentino, on the 19th of February, "have made a fine harvest in Ravenna, Rimini, Pesaro, Ancona, Perugia, Loretto. Said harvest will be instantly forwarded to Paris. Join this to that which will be sent from Rome, and we shall have all that there is of the Beautiful in Italy, except a small number of objects at Naples and Turin."

A sentence ominous of the future for those allies of the French Republic, Turin and Naples.

The reader may not disdain to see the names of the *savants* who reaped harvests of art in the rear of the conqueror's legions. They were the Citizen Monge, Commissary of the Arts and Sciences; and his aids, the Citizens Wicar, painter; Gros, painter; Kreutzer, musician; Marin, sculptor; Gerli, painter; Couturier, secretary, and Moult, agent at Rome. The salary of the assistants was 250 *livres per mensem*. With these few words we take leave of this interesting adjunct to the army of Italy.

Bonaparte quitted Tolentino on the 19th February, stayed some days in Bologna, regulating various matters, and arrived in Mantua on the 2nd of March, there to lay the plans for an offensive campaign in Germany,

Chapter 8

Bonaparte's March into Germany

The French general was now well satisfied with his position in Italy. Venice alone remained in a state of semi-independence, unless Naples, who dared not succour the Pope, be regarded as having any of that precious commodity. But for the destruction of Venice the train was laid, and Bonaparte only waited to choose his own time for firing it.

After the capture of Mantua, he did not go to Milan, because he naively says the inhabitants of Lombardy expected his arrival, and indulged in the hope that he was at length about to permit the union of their primary assemblies. They little thought that their hero was dreaming at times of giving them back to the House of Austria. As to the King of Sardinia, he was willing, seeing nothing better for it, to conclude an offensive and defensive alliance with the Republic, and send a contingent of 10,000 men to Bonaparte, but the Directory did not ratify the treaty signed by Clarke. All was therefore fair, at least on the surface, and it was time to set out on the new campaign.

While he was in the Romagna, Bonaparte had news of the march of reinforcements from the Rhine. The Directory promised to send him 30,000 men, but he estimated that each demi-brigade would lose 500 men on the march, and therefore that the promised 30,000 would be only 19,000 when it reached the Adige. Besides this, the Minister of War deducted 2,000 men to reinforce another French army; and, therefore, the total reinforcements only amounted to 17,000 men. Bonaparte was grateful for this accession of strength, which augmented his army in the field, on the 5th of March, 1797, to 58,474 men.

Massena had under his orders a force of 9,725; Guyeu, acting for Augereau, had a division of 10,215; Serurier and Chabot had 6,543; Bernadotte commanded 6,800; Joubert, 11,625; Rey, 2,500; Dallemagne, 4,600; Victor, 6,466 men. The larger part of the cavalry marched with Augereau. The guns, fifty in number, were unequally divided. Besides this army in the field, the largest Bonaparte had yet commanded, there were 8,706 men in the garrisons of Lombardy, Venetia, Mantua, Piedmont, and Leghorn. Joubert was reinforced by two divisions, which augmented his corps nearly 18,000 men.

On the 10th of March Bonaparte was at Bassano, and thence gave orders for the first operations. The command of the Austrians had been given to the Archduke Charles; and that able officer, destined in after years to contend with Napoleon on the Danube, hastened to the banks of the Piave, and did his utmost to reorganize the wreck of Alvinzi's army, and augment it with fresh troops drawn from the Rhine. But early in March he had not more than 40,000 men covering a great extent of country between the lower Piave and the great road through the Tyrol.

The troops which would have placed him on more than equal terms with his adversary were yet on their march, and would not arrive until April. On the other hand, Bonaparte had assembled all the men he was likely to obtain. Delay would have only strengthened the archduke; and delay never suited the forward spirit of Bonaparte. He, therefore, resolved to take the initiative, and strike at the enemy ere he was prepared. Before putting the army in motion, he issued the following proclamation to "the soldiers of the army of Italy."

Headquarters, Bassano, 10 *Mars*, 1797.
The capture of Mantua has just ended a campaign which gives you an everlasting title to the gratitude of your country. You have gained the victory in fourteen pitched battles and in seventy combats. You have taken more than a hundred thousand prisoners, captured from the enemy

five hundred field pieces, two hundred large cannons, and four pontoons. The contributions exacted from the country you have conquered, have fed, maintained, paid the army, during the whole campaign. You have besides sent thirty millions to the Minister of Finance to add to the public treasury.

You have enriched the Museum of Paris with more than three hundred *chefs-d'œuvre* of ancient and modern Italy. You have conquered for the Republic the finest countries of Europe; the Lombard and Cispadanian Republics owe their liberty to you. French colours float for the first time on the coasts of the Adriatic, opposite to, and twenty-four hours' sail from, ancient Macedonia. The Kings of Sardinia and Naples, the Pope, and the Duke of Parma, have been detached from the coalition of our enemies, and have sued for our alliance. You have driven the English from Leghorn, Genoa, and Corsica.

But you have not yet finished your work. A great destiny is reserved for you; the dearest hopes of our country depend on you; you will continue worthy of them.

Of all the enemies who combined to stifle the Republic at its birth, the Emperor alone remains before us. Degrading himself from the rank of a great power, this prince has become the hireling of the London shopkeepers; he has no policy, no will, but that of those perfidious islanders, who, exempt from the misfortunes of war, smile pleasantly at the miseries of the continent.

The executive Directory has spared nothing to give peace to Europe; the moderation of its propositions did not spring from the strength of its armies; it did not consult your courage, but humanity, and a desire to bring you back to your families. It was not listened to at Vienna. There is, therefore, no other hope of peace than in going to seek it in the heart of the Hereditary Estates of the House of Austria. You will there find a brave people overwhelmed by the late war against the Turks, and by the present war.

The inhabitants of Vienna and the States of Austria groan over the blindness and the despotism of their Government; there is not one among them who is not convinced that English gold has corrupted the Ministers of the Emperor. You will respect their religion and their customs; you will protect their property; you will bring liberty to the brave Hungarian nation.

The House of Austria, which, during three centuries, has gone on losing in every war a part of its power, which renders its subjects discontented by despoiling them of their privileges, will find itself reduced at the end of this sixth campaign (since she obliges us to do it) to accept the peace that we will grant to her, and will descend in reality to the rank of a second-rate power in which she has already placed herself, by receiving the wages, and being at the disposition of England.

Thus prepared, his plan was to carry his army through Friuli, and across the Norique Alps into the valley of the Drave. This accomplished, Joubert was to thrust the Austrians in his front over the high mountains towards Inspruck, enter the valley of the Drave by Brixen, and join Bonaparte. Joubert had conditional orders; but he was desired to move forward on the 18th, when Bonaparte calculated that he should have carried his own army over the Tagliamento—a calculation verified by the result

The campaign was begun by a movement of Massena upon Feltre; Baraguay d'Hilliers, on the right of Joubert, supporting the operation. The snow on the mountains obstructed the march of the divisions, and rain, and wind on the lower ground harassed the soldiers. But Massena passed through Feltre, chasing Lusignan. On the 12th Serurier and Guyeu crossed the Piave, and took post at Conegliano,—Guyeu driving the Austrian advanced guards towards the Tagliamento, and returning on the 13th to Conegliano. Bernadotte, on the extreme right, had moved up to the river from Treviso.

Massena, following the course of the Piave, entered Belluno on the 13th, and, pursuing Lusignan, overtook and surrounded him in the defile of Longarone, and made him and 700 men prisoners. The left was now cleared of enemies, and Massena was ordered to rejoin the main body by crossing the mountains.

On the 13th the whole army was across the Piave, Bernadotte commanding a reserve, a day's march in the rear. Bonaparte, in high spirits, wrote to Massena from Conegliano that the enemy was once more taken *en flagrant délit,* and predicted that everything gave presage of a success which ought to decide the campaign. On the 14th Guyeu was pushed on to Pordenone along the high-road. Serurier followed on the 15th, and Bernadotte was brought up to Sacile. It was from here that Bonaparte expedited the order to Joubert to march on Brixen.

Bonaparte now resolved to pass the Tagliamento on the 16th; and to secure the concentration of his whole force, he ordered Guyeu, who was at Pordenone, to march at five in the morning; Serurier, who was at Pasiamo, to set out at four o'clock; and Bernadotte, who was at Sacile, to march at three o'clock. The whole were to rendezvous at Valvasone, on the right bank of the Tagliamento. Guyeu arrived there at eleven; Bonaparte immediately reconnoitred the enemy's line, and found them strongly posted and entrenched on the left bank. Bernadotte come up at one, and then the action began.

It is remarked that in this battle the army of Italy fought, for the first time, in regular order—the light infantry in front, supported by close columns of grenadiers, and flanked by cavalry. Bonaparte sent Guyeu across the river on his left, to turn the right flank of the Austrians, while Bernadotte moved down the river and attacked the left of the enemy opposite Codriopo. The battle had more of the character of those great conflicts destined to shake Europe in the coming years than any which preceded it The skirmishers dashed through the river in clouds, followed by the dose columns; the artillery was united in masses to protect the points of passage; and the cavalry held in reserve, ready for launching at the right moment.

As the French infantry crossed the stream the Austrian cavalry rode upon them, but, steadily received, they were charged in turn by the French horse and kept off. The Archduke made a counter attack upon the right and left; Bonaparte chose this moment to employ his cavalry reserve, supported by a column of infantry; and their happy charge decided the day. The Austrians fought stoutly, but they were outnumbered, while Bonaparte still held Serurier in reserve. The French artillery played a great part in this battle, and showed itself superior. The French took six guns, a general, and 400 or 500 prisoners.

The Archduke retired behind the Isonzo, and endeavoured to cover the route by Tarvis to Klagenfurth. Resting one day, Bonaparte, on the 18th, seized Palmanuova, and carried all his divisions to that side, except that of Massena, which had taken the important position of Osopo, securing one road, and covering the left of the line. Bonaparte instantly used every effort to convert Palmanuova into a place of strength, to serve as a point of support and a depôt He employed Chasseloup and Lespinasse in this work, and called up the stout old Guillaume from Peschiera to be commandant.

Eager to continue his blows upon the dispirited troops of the Archduke, Bonaparte, having by a happy manoeuvre compelled the garrison of Gradisca to capitulate, placed himself between the Archduke and his right wing under the charge of Ocskay. He had thus, on the 19th, pierced his enemy's line. The Archduke retired on the road to Laybach, followed by Bernadotte; and while Bonaparte hastened up the Isonzo on the track of the Austrian right wing, Massena anticipated them by passing the defiles of Pontebba and occupying Tarvis.

Here Massena was attacked by a body of Austrian reinforcements coming from Klagenfurth; while Guyeu, following Bajalich on the Isonzo, drove him over the mountains towards Massena, who, after defeating his assailants, co-operated with Guyeu in compelling Bajalich and two other generals, with 25 guns, and 2,500 men, to surrender. These combats were carried on among the ice and snow of the Norique Alps, and sometimes above the clouds. The French had entered Germany and Dalmatia. Bonaparte united three divisions at Tarvis. Bernadotte held a position on the road to Laybach, and sent General Dugua to Trieste.

On the 28th, Bonaparte had fixed his head-quarters at Tarvis; and he projected a movement upon Klagenfurth as soon as he should hear that Joubert had reached Botzen. That general received Bonaparte's order to march forward on the 17th. He set out at once from his position in front of Trent, and fighting his way upwards entered Botzen on the 23rd, and Brixen on the 24th. On the 29th, Bonaparte sent Massena towards Klagenfurth, where the Archduke had rallied the remains of his army, but, after a brief combat, the French General entered the town the same evening.

Continuing his daring career, Bonaparte carried his army by Freisach and Neumarkt to Leoben; the Archduke retiring before him, and fighting only with his rear guard. Bernadotte was ordered up to Villach; Joubert was marching down the Drave by Lienz, when the Austrians, alarmed at the proximity of Bonaparte to Vienna, at length consented to his overtures for an armistice. During the negotiations on this subject, the French occupied Gratz and Bruck; and Joubert, after very serious combats with the Tyrolese, effected his junction with the army. On the 18th of April, five weeks after he had marched from Bassano, preliminaries of peace were signed at Leoben.

Undoubtedly, the march of Bonaparte into Germany was one of the most daring of his exploits. It was attended by good fortune, and illustrated by strokes of skill. To the military student, the second volume of his correspondence relating to this enterprise will be found full of instruction.

CHAPTER 9

Campo Formio

The preliminaries of peace signed at Leoben on the 18th of April, arrested the French armies on the Rhine, at length engaged in a forward and triumphant march. The Directory, apparently, at this date, did not desire peace; and what Bonaparte did at Leoben, he did pretty much of his own will.

Both parties agreed to send plenipotentiaries to Berne for the purpose of negotiating a definitive peace. The Emperor gave up the Belgian provinces pertaining to his House. The French promised to evacuate Styria, Carinthia, the Tyrol, Friuli, and Carniola; and compensate the Emperor for the cession of Belgium, The secret articles were far more interesting. The Emperor was to have a large slice of the Venetian territory, the boundaries of which should be the Oglio, the Po, the Adriatic, and his own states. He was also to have Venetian Istria and Dalmatia. Venice was to obtain the Legations, and France the Venetian territory between the Adda, the Oglio, the Po, and the Valteline. French troops were to hold the fortresses until peace was concluded.

On the following day, Bonaparte, foreseeing objections, wrote a long defence of his conduct to the Directory, making the most of its advantages, and showing how easy it would be on some future occasion to recover what was to be given up. He told the Directory that, although his position was brilliant in a military point of view, yet that it was not solid, and that the greatest resistance was sure to be offered to any advance on Vienna.

"If," he said, "at the beginning of the campaign I had

obstinately gone to Turin, I should never have passed the Po; if I had obstinately gone to Borne, I should have lost Milan; and if I had obstinately gone to Vienna, perhaps I should have lost the Republic. . . . You gave me full power over all the diplomatic operations; and in the position of things, the preliminaries of peace even with the Emperor became a military operation. . . . . Calumny strives in vain to impute to me treacherous intentions. My civil career shall be like my military career, one and simple. However, you must fed that I ought to leave Italy, and I urge you to give, with the ratification of the preliminaries, our orders respecting the affairs of Italy, and permission for me to return to France."

This threat of resignation was used later with effect Bonaparte knew the danger of his position, and was right in saying that he did not dictate a peace. Joubert had narrowly escaped from the Tyrol, which was closed behind him. Loudon, finding the road open, had marched down the Adige, and had assisted in an insurrection which broke out in Venetia. The intrigues of the French had called forth a democratic sedition in Brescia and Bergamo, and the peasants and aristocratic party had made a counterplot. The Polish and Lombard Legions helped the democrats, and the Venetian troops, assisted by Loudon, opposed them.

The insurgents selected a French officer to be their commander; and civil war raged between the Oglio and the Adige. The French were massacred in the streets of Verona, and the troops there were besieged in the castle. But Loudon, hearing of the first armistice at Leoben, withdrew into the Tyrol, and Kilmaine, collecting the French garrisons, raised the siege, and recaptured the town. The French took ample vengeance. The ringleaders of the Venetian patriots were shot; some houses were sacked, and the town had to pay 1,800,000 *francs*.

Bonaparte withdrew his army as fast as he could; from the sterile mountains of Germany, and posted them in the Venetian States. He affected to show thereby his respect for the Emperor; his real motive was the troubles in his rear. Of these troubles he made an able use. For Venice, having thus given him a pretext for which he had long been waiting, and the pretext occurring at a moment when he could I dispose of his army, by the agency of the French Legation he plotted a democratic revolution in Venice; and the "most ridiculous and oppressive of all governments" being suddenly overturned, he sent a body of troops to sustain the democrats; and thus, without the loss of a man, obtained possession of a city which, forewarned, would have defied a siege.

A month after the preliminaries of Leoben were signed, a French general was quartered in the palaces of the Queen of the Adriatic; a French division domineered in its watery streets; and a provisional government played at independence in the halls of St. Mark. Bonaparte intended to reserve Venice as a bait for Austria. In his inscrutable mind the doom of that ancient Republic and the fate of its people had long been sealed. The day had now come; and the Republic of Venice was among the things that were.

But negotiations made no progress. Austria, hoping much from the plots of the French Royalists in Paris, held back, and threw obstacles in the way of peace. The Congress never met at Berne. Bonaparte himself went to Milan, to bring Genoa under the yoke of France, and to organize the Italian republics. He annexed Modena, Reggio, Bergamo, Ferrara, Bologna, to the Cisalpine Republic, to show Austria that he intended to keep fast hold of these. French influence had raised a revolt at Genoa; and, although the Genoese patricians fought more stoutly for their privileges than those of Venice, and conquered for a moment, yet they submitted to the mediation of Bonaparte, who favoured first a moderate constitutional reform, and next named a provisional government The democrats then broke forth, burned the golden book, dashed in pieces the statues of Doria, and committed other excesses. The object of France was obtained: Genoa was no longer independent, but a gate into Italy, garrisoned by the French.

It does not enter into the plan of this work to describe the struggle of parties in Paris which ended in the *coup d'état* of the *18 fructidor*, or 3rd of August, when the Directory, or rather three of its members, caused an armed force to invade the Chamber of the Legislative Councils, and arrest those members who were plotting with the emigrants and royalists to overturn the Republic.

Bonaparte contributed his share to this *coup d'état* by sending Augereau to Paris, and pouring in threatening addresses from the army, levelled at Pichegru, Willot, and the Royalists. "Tremble, royalists!" he said; "from the Adige to the Seine is but one step." Augereau was the sword of this measure of violence, which frustrated the hopes founded by Austria upon the plots of the counter-revolutionists. They were arrested, and many were sent to Cayenne, or rather ordered to be transported thither, for many did not leave the Isle of Ré.

The Directory, triumphant in Park, was jealous of the chief of the army of Italy, whose astucity they had felt, whose character they could not penetrate, whose designs they could not fathom, whose professions they did not trust. Bonaparte was negotiating at Passeriano, and, says Bourrienne, "Augereau and the Directory filled Passeriano with spies." Bonaparte took it up brusquely, and, telling them they treated him almost as if he were Pichegru, requested them to accept his resignation.

> "For a long time," he wrote, "you have confided a great power to me; I have always used it for the good of the country. So much the worse for those who do not believe in virtue, and who may have suspected mine. My reward is in my conscience and the opinion of posterity."

The Directory hastened to assure him of their confidence, and to compliment him on his respect for the civil powers.

The great divergences of opinion among the negotiators were at length reconciled. Venice, which had been called to freedom, paid the cost.

> "One morning in October," says Bourrienne, "on opening my windows at daybreak, I saw that the mountains were

covered with snow. The evening before was superb, and the autumn promised to be fine and protracted. I entered the chamber of the General, as usual, at seven o'clock; I woke him and told him what I had seen. At first he pretended to disbelieve me, jumped out of bed and ran to the window to witness the change for himself. Then, slowly and calmly, he said, 'Before the middle of October! What a country! Come, we must make peace.'

"He went into his cabinet, and reviewed, with the greatest care, the state of his army, and said, 'See, I have nearly 80,000 effective. I feed them, I pay them; but I should not have 60,000 in the day of battle. I should win; but I should have in killed, wounded, and prisoners, 20,000 less. How could I resist all the Austrian forces that would march to succour Vienna. The armies of the Rhine, even if they are ready, could not second me under a month, and in fifteen days the snow will block up the passes of the mountains. It is finished; I will make peace. Venice shall pay for the war and the limit of the Rhine. Let the Directory and the lawyers say what they please.'"

This was on the 13th of October; on the 17th the treaty was signed at Campo Formio. The Directory was dissatisfied, and said it was not making peace, it was adjourning war. But they might say what they pleased; they could do nothing. By the treaty of Campo Formio, France gained Belgium, and Mayence, and Mantua. Venice, Legnago, Peschiera, Verona, with the territory, on the left bank of the Adige, Istria, Dalmatia, Friuli—in short, all that belonged to the ancient republic east of the Adige were given to Austria; and she recognized the Rhine and the Alps as the limits of France Proper. France also obtained the Ionian Islands, hitherto Venetian. Brescia and Bergamo were added to the Cisalpine Republic, which was recognized by the Emperor.

A number of secret articles were appended to the treaty, wherein Austria and France, for their own profit, undertook to compel other powers to give and take in Germany, in order to carry out the great French idea of a Rhine frontier. A congress was to meet at Radstadt to finally settle these affairs.

Before the year expired the Directory had revolutionized and despoiled Switzerland; revolutionized and despoiled Rome. Early in 1798 Berthier, at the head of two divisions, entered Rome, and the people declared themselves free. The Pope, Pius VI., abdicated, on the 15th of February, the twenty-fifth anniversary of his Pontificate; and three days afterwards, says Jomini, as a thanksgiving for the abolition of his sovereignty and the establishment of the Roman Republic, a solemn *Te Deum* was chanted in the church of St. Peter by fourteen cardinals! The Pope left Rome on the 20th, and retired to Pisa, where he remained until he was transferred to France.

In leaving Italy free and independent, Bonaparte left behind him an army of 30,000 Frenchmen, who were maintained at the expense of the Italian Republic, to preserve its freedom and defend its independence. He went to Radstadt, and, finding that the atmosphere of diplomacy did not agree with him, returned to Paris. Let Jomini recount what Italy had to pay for her liberation:—

> More than 120,000,000 of extraordinary contributions had been levied in Italy; 60,000,000 had paid, fed, and reorganized the army of Italy; 60,000,000 sent to the Treasury at Paris, had aided it in providing for the wants of the Interior and the services of the army on the, Rhine. Besides this important assistance, the Treasury owed to the victories of Bonaparte an annual saving of 70,000,000, the sum which, in 1796, was applied to the maintenance of the armies of the Alps and of Italy. Quantities of hemp and timber, vessels seized at Genoa, Leghorn, Venice, had restored the marine at Toulon. The National Museum was enriched with the master-pieces of art which had embellished Parma, Florence, and Rome, and which were valued at 200,000,000.

But Italians tell us that their freedom was cheap at the price, because the French conquest sowed the seeds of national life. They are the best judges.

PART 2

CAMPAIGN OF MARENGO 1800

CHAPTER 1

Army of Reserve

Bonaparte had been in Egypt, seeking glory, and dreaming of an Eastern empire. Fortune had not favoured him in this arid clime. He had taken Malta, he had occupied the valley of the Nile and scattered the Mamelukes, but he had also seen, with mingled rage and admiration, the application of his own principles of war, by a genius not inferior to his own, to the destruction of his fleet in the Bay of Aboukir, and he had been himself defeated at Acre, by the firmness and courage of a Turkish Pasha and an English sailor. Sidney Smith had sent Bonaparte a French journal in June 1799; and he read in its pages enough to show him that the Italy he had so painfully conquered had been torn from the grasp of the French.

Sick of Eastern adventure, he resolved to quit Egypt, and return to push his fortunes in Europe. Stealing away, without informing his army or his comrades, he embarked at Alexandria on the 23rd August; by skill as much as luck, he evaded the English cruisers, and landed at Fréjus on the 8th October, 1799, a year and five months after he had embarked for Egypt at Toulon. In a few days he astonished the Directory by suddenly appearing in Paris.

During his absence how much had happened! The Congress at Radstadt had led to war. Austria had declined to submit to the propositions of the Directory, and Russia and England had rallied to her side. Once more a coalition rose up to contest with France her pretension to supremacy in Europe. Nelson's victory of the Nile fixed their resolves. All Italy south of the Po and west of the Adige was under the dominion of the French, organized in republics, nominally independent, but actually writhing under the oppressions of military proconsuls, whose authority was enforced, by the bayonets and sabres of 116,000 protectors. In like manner Switzerland had succumbed, but the smaller cantons still showed a spirit of resistance; and the Directory, it has teen sarcastically remarked, thought it very shocking that the descendants of Tell should believe themselves to be freer than the Jacobins.

The struggle began on all sides early in 1799, the French leading the way. But they were not this time destined to be victorious. In a few months the armies they had sent into Germany were driven back across the Rhine. The feeble, generals, who commanded in Italy, scattered over a large territory, were beaten in detail. The Austrian Kray, crossing the Adige, blockaded Mantua; and the Russian Suwaroff pushed on to Turin, thrusting the French towards Alessandria. Macdonald, coming up from Naples and Tuscany, was assailed by Suwaroff in the valley of the Trebbia and put to the rout Massena, in the meantime, had bravely made head in Switzerland; but the French were defeated on all other points, and only held Genoa, Mantua, and a few strong places in Italy.

The Directory, to restore its affairs, raised a new army, and sent the gallant Joubert to command it Joubert, moved up from. Genoa, and opposed by Kray, who had taken Mantua, and by Suwaroff, met death and defeat at Novi. Massena still held on in Switzerland, and he had the good fortune to defeat the Russians at Zurich before Suwaroff could come up, and compelled that able general, who had crossed the St Gothard, to retreat with all speed into Bavaria. The French, in September, made a last effort to relieve Coni, besieged by Mélas, but they miserably failed. The hand of the master was wanting; and in Holland and Switzerland alone were the French victorious. It cannot be doubted, now, that when Bonaparte returned to France, the people of all classes were seething with rage against the Directory, which had known neither how to conquer, nor how to keep what others had conquered, nor how to unite internal order with external strength, nor how to reconcile liberty and law.

The name of Bonaparte had never been associated with misfortune abroad, or misgovernment at home. He came from his journey in the East, clothed, to the popular eye, with something of the splendour that has always surrounded Eastern conquerors. The people knew not the truth. They only knew that he who had conquered Italy and marched into Germany was once more on the soil of France; and they believed all the lying stories of the glory of the Egyptian campaign. The flight of Bonaparte from Alexandria even seemed a noble action. For had not this invincible soldier rushed to defend his adopted country, and had he not arrived when his presence was sorely needed? Was he not also *le héros des idées libérales?*

His advent in Paris, therefore, was the signal for a revolution. It is not our business to describe the machinery set in motion to produce the famous *coup d'état,* of the *18th Brumaire* (9th November). It is sufficient to say that Bonaparte, invested with military power, seized an occasion so favourable to his views, practically made himself Dictator of France, under the title of First Consul, and never relaxed his grasp of power until united Europe wrenched it from him. By the sword he won it, and by the sword he lost it. When a man is everything, it has been said, everything falls when he falls; and when the destiny of a nation depends on the gain or the loss of a battle, it depends on nothing.

Arrived at power, Bonaparte made an effort to detach England from Austria. He offered a separate peace to each; he only desired to make peace with one. He desired to conclude a peace with that Power which the more easily fell into the snare, and immediately to fall upon the other. He would have preferred peace with England; because, deprived of English gold, Austria would have been more easily overthrown. England refused to make a separate peace; and Austria gave a like response. There was then nothing for it but war. For this he prepared the nation; and for this he animated the soldiers:—

"Soldiers !" he said, "in promising peace to the French people, I have been your organ; I know your valour.

"You are the same men who conquered Holland, the Rhine, Italy, and who made peace under the walls of Vienna.

"Soldiers! it is not your own frontiers that you have now to defend; it is the enemy's States that you must now invade.

"There are none of you who have not gone through several campaigns; who do not know that the most essential quality of a soldier is to know how to hear privations with patience. Several years of mal-administration cannot be repaired in a single day.

"As the First Magistrate of the Republic, it will be a great pleasure to me to make the whole nation know the corps who, by their discipline and their valour, merit to be proclaimed as the bulwarks of our country.

"Soldiers! when the right time comes, I will be in the midst of you; and astonished Europe shall remember that you are of the race of the brave."

In the spring of 1800, Bonaparte determined to make war both on the Rhine and in Italy. He also resolved, although the laws forbade it, to lead, himself, the army destined to recover his Italian conquests. He induced Moreau to take command of the Army of the Rhine; and that able, but unfortunate soldier, though fortunate in this case, had, early in May, driven the Austrians into Ulm. Massena, perhaps then the ablest of the lieutenants of the great captain, took command of the Army of Italy. The Austrian General, Mélas, succeeded in driving Massena, with, one part of the army, into Genoa, and forcing Suchet, with the other, over the Var; but he did not himself manage to cross that frontier stream.

He remained at Vintimiglia, while Ott blockaded Massena in Genoa; and the rest of the magnificent force, under the orders of Mélas, was divided into small parties, and posted in the many passes leading from France and Switzerland into Italy. Bonaparte determined to deliver Genoa; and in older to effect this, he conceived and executed what will always be regarded as one of the most extraordinary exploits in his career. He resolved to cross the Alps, and fall upon the rear of the Austrians.

"On the 17th of March," says Bourrienne, "in a moment of gaiety and good humour, he made me unroll the great map of Italy. Then, with great attention, he stuck into the map a set of pins, some having on their heads red, and some white wax. I looked on, and waited the result of this inoffensive campaign in profound silence. When he had placed the enemy's corps, and the red pins on the points where he hoped to conduct his troops, he said,—'Where do you think I shall fight Mélas?'—

"'The devil take me if I know anything about it'—

"'You are a simpleton. Look here. Mélas is at Alessandria, where he has his head-quarters. He will remain there until Genoa is taken. In Alessandria he has his artillery, his magazines, his hospitals, his reserves. Passing the Alps here,' (pointing to the Great St Bernard), 'I shall fall upon Mélas, and cut off his communications with Austria; and I shall fight him here, in the plains of the Scrivia,' placing a red pin at San Giuliano.'"

Bourrienne tells us that he soon forgot all about this pastime, as he thought the manoeuvres with the pins. But three months afterwards, he reminded Bonaparte, on the spot, a few hours after the victory of Marengo, of the scene in the cabinet of the First Consul at the Tuileries.

That he might execute this plan, so lightly regarded by his civilian secretary, Bonaparte formed an Army of Reserve.

"The problem," says Colonel Macdougall in his *Theory*

of War, was how to conceal from the numerous spies of England and Austria the assembly and movement of such an army. Napoleon judged that the best way to effect Ins object was himself to divulge its existence with such ostentation as to excite the ridicule of his enemies when collated with the apparent facts; so that they might be fed to consider the pompous announcement of its strength as merely an attempt to create a diversion in favour of Massena, who was blockaded and starving in Genoa.

"In order to direct the attention of the spies to a definite point, Dijon was named as the rendezvous of the army. All the spies flocked to that place and witnessed the pompous review of about 8,000 half-armed and badly-clothed conscripts by Napoleon in person, in the beginning of May. All Europe immediately rang with ridicule of 'Bonaparte's army of reserve.'

"At the same time that the formation of this army was published with the greatest ostentation, Napoleon caused numerous handbills to be printed, in which, interspersed with many scandalous anecdotes of the First Consul and his Court, pretended proofs were given of the impossibility of the existence of 'the Army of Reserve.' Meanwhile, the divisions of the real army of reserve, which numbered 36,000 men and 40 guns, had been secretly assembled at different points along its intended route.

"It was principally composed of old soldiers drawn from La Vendée, which the conciliatory measures of Napoleon had pacified. Its advanced guard was reviewed by him at Lausanne on the 13th May, and it was in full march for Italy at the very moment when the Austrians before Genoa were saying that the French counted too much on their gullibility in hoping to induce them to raise the siege of Genoa by the fear of being attacked by an army of 8,000 invalids and conscripts."

Yet the precious secret, so studiously guarded, was in peril of being suddenly revealed; for a despatch to Massena, giving full details, had been entrusted to Reille, who, evading the British cruisers, carried it safely to Genoa.

Bonaparte meditated the passage of the Alps at four points. He was to lead himself the main body over the Great St. Bernard, and with admirable forethought, he sent a good round sum of money to the hospitable monks, in order that they might have provisions in readiness for his men. A second column, under Chabran, was to cross the Little St. Bernard; a third, under Moncey, detached from Lecourbe's division, then part of the right wing of the army of the Rhine, was ordered to pass over the St. Gothard; and a fourth column had instructions to take the road over the Simplon. That his enemies might be further deceived, the army in Dauphiny was to push several small bodies through the passes of the Western Alps. The plan was bold, hazardous, incredible; it was precisely the kind of movement which no enemy could foresee; and in its daring and improbability lay the safety of its projector.

The Austrians were in part scattered all over the inner side of the great mountain barrier, looking for anything rather than an army descending from the snows. Mélas had eyes only for Genoa and the Var. His lieutenants were at the foot of the St Gothard, at the gorge of the Simplon in the valley of Aosta, at Susa, Pigneroli, and Coni; the greater part of their fine and numerous army being before Genoa and in the pleasant slopes of the Maritime Alps. This was precisely what the First Consul desired; and he counted upon their remaining in their isolated positions, until he could leap into their midst.

The possession of Switzerland, it will be seen at a glance, enabled the French military chief to carry out his plan. The mountain ridges covered all his movements, and it seemed for more likely that he would appear in Germany than in Italy.

Bonaparte quitted Paris on the 6th of May, saying that he should return in fifteen days—he was really absent only fifty-seven; and in the interval how much had he not done! In the middle of May he was at Martigny, and his columns were already climbing up the steeps of the Mont St. Bernard. The Army of Reserve was on the march for the plains of Scrivia, and its mighty leader was dreaming of the place he should fill in history beside Alexander, Caesar, and Hannibal.

CHAPTER 2

The Passage of the Alps

Once on the march, with a great plan to execute, a great object to gain, Bonaparte was not the man to brook delay. He went forth confident of victory; an adorer of fortune, but a devotee also of prudence. Conscious of his genius for war and politics, he was athirst for power and the glory that crowns him who wins power by the combined force of strong will and a sharp sword obedient to an almost unerring eye. He had conquered Italy; he had quitted her fertile plains, and left her noble people practically the servants of France, and he had gone to seek in the East a new career. He had returned to find his conquest reversed, and he burned with the desire of showing that he could conquer again.

But not alone for the glory to be won in uniting Italy once more to France, did he send his legions over the snowy summits of the Alps. He had a greater object, a stronger passion, a more forecasting intent Bonaparte resolved to be a conqueror once more upon the plans of Italy, in order that he might with the swift and sturdy blows of victory strike the foundations of his power deeper into the soil of France. Glory he loved, but glory as the gilding of power. Power he loved for its own sake, and as a means of gathering more glory. And thus, when detained in the dreary village of Martigny, looking ever upward to catch sight of the couriers who should bring him news of the first success, his dream was, of the victories he should win, and of the power he should build upon them when he returned to *his* beautiful

France.

The Austrians were reposing on their triumphs of 1799, and the sounds of war were unheard, except around the fortress of Genoa, where Massena so heroically kept them at bay, when the leading sections of Bonaparte's columns strode forth to scale the Alps. On the 17th of May, Lannes, destined to reap such a harvest of fame in this short campaign, led the advanced guard up the winding road towards the realm of snow. The main column, gay and eager, marched up the stupendous barrier. The cannons were taken off their carriages, placed in trucks or blocks of wood hollowed out to receive them, and dragged along by main force. The baggage was carried over.

Upwards went the hardy throng, laughing at fatigue, overcoming obstacles, gay and sportive within the reach of, the dread avalanche, or on the brink of precipice and chasm. The French soldier is quick to perceive, and he must have felt that he was engaged in an enterprise that the world would admire, and the feeling must have given wings to his feet, strength to his arm, and lightness to his burdens. As the grenadiers, with Lannes at their head, who, four years before, had conducted them in that rapid march upon Piacenza which opened the gate of Lombardy to their young chief,—as these hardy soldiers reached the mountain crest, they flung their hats into the clear air, and woke the echoes with shouts that had not been heard in those frozen regions since Hannibal's African and Spanish Infantry awoke like echoes in a tongue now dead, in their painful march towards the smiling valley of Aosta.

Bonaparte's foresight now served him well, for the monks of St. Bernard, who had never before seen such a strange host of visitants, laid before them the bread and cheese and wine provided by the fostering care of their leader. Their natural strength revived, these hardy warriors once more caught up their arms, resumed their labours, and their lengthened line stretched far down the rocky road, their backs to the snow, and their faces towards that blooming land, whose corn and wine and oil, whose material and spiritual wealth, have ever proved such powerful attractions to the Gallic people.

As the main torrent of soldiers came down from the snows of the Great St. Bernard, the tributary streams from the Little St. Bernard, who had followed Hannibal's road, poured down also into the valley of the Dora Baltea; and, on the east, other affluents came from the Simplon and the battle-swept crags of St. Gothard, to unite their strength with the main body in the plains of Milan. The Austrians still mounted guard in unsuspecting quietude in the valleys under the Alpine rampart, when these armed hosts descended from the clouds to destroy them in detail.

Napoleon had forgotten one thing; but that one oversight, fatal to an ordinary man, only served to bring out his faculty for illustrating the famous definition of a difficulty—a thing, to be overcome. The French soldiers marching proudly down the beautiful valley of Aosta were suddenly brought to a stand by the Fort of Bard. Standing across the outlet from the valley of Aosta, where the long, and ragged spurs, shot out from the Monte Rosa on one side and the Mont Iseran on the other, almost meet, the Fort of Bard is a fortified gateway into the valley. The roads from the Great and Little St. Bernard meet at the ancient city of Aosta, and thenceforth, like the Dora itself, seek through that defile an issue into the plain.

Warned by the expulsion of his outpost at Chatillon that a French corps had crossed the Alps, the governor of the Fort of Bard resolutely opposed the further progress of the army. Thus Bonaparte's whole centre force was arrested and chafing like a caged lion. There was no other outlet, except that through Bard, unless the skill of the general found one. It was the delay in capturing this little fort that caused Bonaparte to linger a prey to *ennui* at Martigny.

Tired out at length, he hurried over the Great St. Bernard. "He wore his grey frock coat," says Bourrienne, "and he walked with his horsewhip in his hand, in a somewhat melancholy mood, because none brought him news of the surrender of the fort of Bard." Had he been with the advance, perhaps this fort would have caused no delay, for it was found that the infantry, with great labour, could climb the heights of Albaredo, one of the spurs of the Monte Rosa, that fold, in the valley, and thus turn the fort. But another and greater difficulty remained. Though foot, soldiers could scale the mountain, horse and cannon could not follow them. Bonaparte then cut a road over the rocks for his horsemen, and carried forward his guns, as Wellington, twelve years afterwards, at Burgos, carried his off, within range of the fort.

The little town of Bard was in the hands of the French,, and under the guns of the fort; but, choosing the night, and wrapping straw round the wheels of the carriages and tumbrils, and covering the hoofs of the horses, thus illustrating King Lear's great stratagem, they transported their artillery safely through. Then, leaving this little obstacle behind him to the care of a small besieging force, whose operations he dictated, he rode into Ivrea, where Lannes had already taken up his quarters. Thus, on the 23rd of May, the two columns which had swarmed down the St. Bernard mountain, united into one, debouched into the plains of Piedmont.

The Austrians were surprised and bewildered. Bonaparte, to distract the attention of Mélas, had ordered Thureau to show small columns in all the principal passes of the Western Alps. In an address to France, calling for volunteers to swell the ranks of the army of reserve, the First Consul had adroitly hinted at invasion by the Mont Cénis road, thus playing again the card which had proved trumps in the armistice of Cherasco—the stipulation for a passage of the Po at Valenza. Mélas looked to the Western Alps; and when Bonaparte was at Ivrea on the Dora Baltea, Mélas was at Savigliano, with his face towards France.

Thus, when Bonaparte was about to unite 60,000 men in Lombardy, out of the immense force under the command of Mélas, that general could not muster more than 18,000 Austrians to oppose him, nor were these united. They were divided into small parties between the head of the Lago Maggiore and Turin. Already the column of Moncey was marching down the valley of the Upper Ticino by Bellinzona, on the east of the Lago Maggiore, and the column which had crossed the Simplon was on its western brink, blockading Arona. The Austrian troops were falling one after the other under the blows of superior numbers; and their general was far from guessing at his enemy's design.

Quitting Ivrea, Bonaparte directed Lannes upon Chivasso, to cover the right of his line of march. On hearing from the fugitives, who had been expelled from the valley of Aosta, that the French were at hand, the Austrian Haddick occupied a camp at Chiusella, and endeavoured to defend the bridge there over the Dora Baltea. Lannes overthrew him, drove him towards Turin, and followed as far as Chivasso. Bonaparte's object was to induce the enemy to believe that he intended to march on Turin, while he really intended to move upon Milan. This was his masterstroke. For this he had passed the Alps. Instead of seeking to fight Mélas in the heart of Piedmont, he bent his energies to the task of seizing all the communications of his foes.

In the meantime, three small French columns, issuing through the passes of the Western Alps, were amusing the Austrians by daring advances and sudden retreats, and compelling them to keep their eyes fixed on Mont Cénis and Mont Genevre. In fact, French columns seemed to be rushing from the mountains on all sides, and Mélas may be excused under such circumstances for not having perceived the drift of all these apparently eccentric and disjointed manoeuvres. The siege of Genoa made progress, in spite of the tenacity and ingenuity of Massena; Sachet did not stir; all combined to delude Mélas, who, the year before, had found no difficulty in repelling a series of widespread and isolated attempts to drive him from the Stura.

Bonaparte had lost no time at Ivrea. Starting at once, he inarched along the great basin of Piedmont through those towns whose names are now so familiar to our ears—Santhia, San Germano, Vercelli, Novara. Murat, who now commanded his advanced guard, forced the passage of the Ticino at Turbigo (where another Bonaparte has recently crossed that river), defeating

Loudon, who had gathered up a few men to defend it, and forcing Wukassowich, who had come down from the upper valley, to seek safety with Loudon behind the Mincio Lannes, taking the road along the left bank of the Po, brought the rear-guard by Crescentino, Trino, Mortara, to the banks of the Ticino, and crossing it there, took Pavia and a siege train.

Moncey came down from the Alpine regions into the Milanese; on the 2nd of June, Bonaparte was once more in Milan itself, and in a few days he was master of the line of the Adda from Lodi to the Po. The fort of Bard was also taken, and the line of communications with Switzerland secured, Massena held out in Genoa, but he was not destined to do so for long.

Bonaparte's first care was to make good the ground he had won. So careful was he to preserve that necessary of life to a general, a line of retreat, that he remained four days in Milan for the purpose of securing it; and enfeebled his army to cover his rear from possible attacks on the side of the Mincio. He therefore held a line of communications between Ivrea and Milan, placed a division in Pavia and Milan, sent troops as far as Crema and Brescia, and blockaded Pizzighettone and the castle of Piacenza. Thus, although he had brought above 60,000 men into Italy, he had not more than 32,000 with which to realise the plan, sketched with coloured pins in the Tuileries, and to fall upon the Austrians, if they were willing to fight, in the valley of the Scrivia.

Mélas had now become alive to the danger which menaced him, and he took energetic steps to ward it off. Elsnitz, the officer commanding on the Var, was ordered up to Alessandria by the valley of the Tanaro, and he began his retrograde movement at the end of May; but Suchet, following quickly, and manoeuvring with his left, cut him off from the pass of Tenda, by seizing the defile of Saorgio and separating his enemy's corps, he drove some over the Apennines, and others along the Corniche. Suchet advanced to Savona, and the Austrians retired over the hills.

The object of Suchet's manoeuvres and combats was to carry

succour to Massena, who had been holding out resolutely in Genoa, beset on land by the Austrian Ott, and on the sea face of his stronghold by the Briton Keith. Massena had made a magnificent defence, fighting valiantly with a starving garrison. Ott had made many advances towards a capitulation; but, unable to agree to his terms, Massena would have cut his way out of the place on the side of Spezia, to join the army of reserve, had not this desperate measure been rejected by his brigadiers.

Better succour was at hand. The advance of the army of reserve into Lombardy, the successes of Suchet, had made Mélas anxious that Ott's corps should be at his side. He therefore ordered Ott to make the best terms he could with Massena, and join the main body at Alessandria without loss of time; giving him as a reason for this step an account of the astounding proceedings of the French. Ott accordingly entered into negotiations with Massena, but he found the Frenchman so stout of heart, so imperious even, that he was compelled to permit the garrison to evacuate Genoa with arms, artillery, baggage; one part of the garrison to march by Voltri to join Suchet, the other to be transferred in English ships to Antibes. The Austrian was forced, by the exigencies of his situation and the vehemence of Massena, to sign the capitulation on the 3rd of June, the day after Bonaparte entered Milan.

CHAPTER 3

The Battle of Marengo

Mélas was now in that position which is the most certain to lead to disaster in war: the enemy was in possession of all his communications. The Austrian General was quite cut off from Vienna. Even his couriers were intercepted by the French; and it was from a capture of the despatches carried by one of them that Bonaparte first heard of the capitulation of Genoa. Bonaparte's march on Milan gave him the whole of Lombardy at a blow; and by the 6th of June the French outposts were as far to the east as Brescia, and the discomfited columns of Loudon and Wukasso-wich had only felt themselves in safety on the Mincio.

All the magazines in these countries fell into the hands of the French, and Mélas had to depend entirely upon the stores in Alessandria, which Bonaparte learned from a double spy at Milan were but scant. Nor was this all. The petty detachments which had skirmished in the Western Alps had detained Austrian troops to watch them, and so far enfeebled the main body. Suchet's hardy pursuit of Elsnitz had cost that officer thousands of men, and had compelled him to distribute widely those who remained.

Ott also had to weaken his corps in order to garrison Genoa; and thus, of the immense army which Mélas had commanded at the beginning of June, estimated at nearly 100,000 men, he could only unite in Alessandria for battle some 24,000 foot and 8,000 horse. Early in June, he did not believe in the existence of the army of reserve led on by Bonaparte; he was now only too finally convinced of its dangerous proximity.

Bonaparte, on the other hand, remained six days in Milan, taking measures to secure his communications, and restore the political ascendancy of France in Lombardy. On the night of the 8th of June, he received the letter from Mélas to the Aulic Council, which Mural captured at Piacenza. The news of the surrender of Genoa seems to have determined him to march at once upon the enemy. Lannes, with the advanced guard, had already crossed the Po at San Cipriano, and had occupied for two days the position of Stradella; Murat, crossing near Piacenza, was close at hand; and, on the 9th, Bonaparte himself hastened to Stradella in advance of his main body. He left Moncey, with part of the troops that general had brought over the St Gothard, from the left wing of Moreau's army, to blockade the castle of Milan, and keep all safe in that quarter. By transferring his army to the right bank of the Po, Bonaparte gained a new line of retreat in case of a reverse, for he might have fallen back upon Tuscany, and have drawn to him the detachments in Lombardy.

On the 9th, his troops had not all passed the Po, which, suddenly rising, an occurrence not unusual in streams fed from mountain sources, had broken his bridge, and had detained on the Lombard bank a large part of the infantry, and nearly all the cavalry. Nevertheless, Lannes was sent on towards Voghera with his division. The road from Stradella to Voghera runs along the lower slopes of the Apennines, where they subside towards the Po, and passes through Casteggio and Montebello, names again rendered familiar to English ears by the victorious combat wherein another French general has defeated an Austrian.

While Lannes was marching up from Stradella, Ott, with his corps diminished by the strong garrison he had thrown into Genoa, instead of joining his chief at Alessandria, crossed the hills, and marched towards Voghera, with about 14,000 men, in the hope of anticipating Bonaparte at Stradella, and of preventing him from crossing the Po. This was a false movement; because it was of the last importance that the greatest possible number of men should be assembled at Alessandria in the shortest possible time. Ott judged otherwise, and therefore he moved his corps so far from all support. The consequences were evil ones for him. We always pay for our mistakes, and never more dearly than in war. The march of Ott towards Stradella led to the combat at Montebello.

Lannes, marching up the road, had anticipated the Austrian, and encountered him at Montebello. The gallant Frenchman, although he had with him not more than 6,000 men, was not inclined to retire. The Austrian fell on with vigour. Lannes defended himself with great constancy, but the odds were against him. Always hardy, he held fast to the heights, and even tried to fall on the flank of his opponent. Yet he must have given way before overwhelming numbers, had not Victor brought up Gardanne's division to his aid. With this reinforcement Lannes soon changed probable defeat into certain victory.

Ott, assailed on both flanks by French soldiers, conducted by men like Lannes, Victor, and Gardanne, was broken, and almost destroyed. When he hurried back on the road to Alessandria, he left behind him many hundreds dead, or wounded, or prisoners, and five guns. The happy issue of the combat of Montebello gained for Lannes in after years a title, when France was endowed with a military aristocracy, and thrones and titles were once more in vogue. The combat of Montebello was regarded as the harbinger of a greater victory, and the spirits of the army were exalted to a high pitch by this instalment of glory. Nor were the solid advantages less; for Lannes had thus opened for Bonaparte a clear road to Marengo.

Bonaparte had now united his army on the south of the Po, and he marched forward to seek his opponent at his point of concentration, Alessandria. The prediction he had made to Bourrienne at the Tuileries in March was about to be accomplished. By a happy chance he had been joined at Stradella, on the 11th, by Desaix, one of his most prized comrades in arms. Desaix had, on arriving from Egypt at Toulon, written to Paris to say that he had returned, and that he desired nothing better than to take the field at the earliest moment. Bonaparte heard of this at Martigny, and immediately called Desaix to the army of reserve. This brave officer lost no time in rejoining his chief, who valued him as a soldier and loved him as a man, if, indeed, Bonaparte ever loved any one. Desaix was worth much, and Bonaparte immediately gave him the command of his centre divisions.

The French army marched along the road by Voghera towards Alessandria, and, crossing the Scrivia, entered the plains of Marengo; Gardanne, with the advance, crossing on the 12th of June. The army of Mélas was posted behind the Bormida, within and in front of the fortress. Alessandria stands in an angle formed by the junction of two rivers, the Tanaro and the Bormida, where these rivers, swollen by many streams, flow from the high ground into a vast plain, "enclosed on one side by the Montferrat hills,, and on the other by the outskirts of the Apennines of Novi, Tortona, and Voghera."

It has always been a place of strength. In 1168 the Lombard League selected it as the site of their chief stronghold, when menaced by the warriors of Germany; Napoleon, nearly seven centuries after, confirmed the judgment of the Lombards; and in our day La Marmora and the Piedmontese school of war have adopted the views, and profited by the sagacity of the first French Emperor. In 1800 it was a powerful fortress, covered by one river and seated astride of the other, and well adapted to support and conceal the assembling of an army. Mélas was here posted, uncertain what course to take, and stunned by the heavy blow which had fallen upon him in the midst, of such seeming good fortune, when Bonaparte brought up his brigades in front of the Bormida.

The First Consul had all along been apprehensive lest Mélas should escape him. In his *Memoirs* dictated at St Helena—memoirs not always nor often to be trusted—he describes three courses which he assumes were open to the Austrian. One was to attack and overthrow the French, while he was superior in number. A second was to pass the Po above Casale, and hasten by forced marches over the Ticino, and, overthrowing the French detachments in Lombardy, reach the line of the Adda. A third was to march by Novi upon Genoa, take post upon the Apennines above, and, before he resumed the offensive, await there the arrival of an English force, which Bonaparte supposed to be ready to sail from Minorca. It was this course which the First Consul feared Mélas would adopt; and he approached Marengo under the impression that the enemy, hidden from his view by the walls of Alessandria, was engaged in some manoeuvre to outwit and escape him.

On the 13th he crossed the Scrivia, and entered the plain of Marengo. No enemy was visible. A few horsemen watched from afar, but the Austrian army was not posted on a plain so favourable for the movements of an arm in which they were superior, the cavalry. Eager to know whether Mélas had marched on Genoa, Bonaparte directed Desaix to move to the left towards Novi, and watch the road that ran from Novi to Alessandria. At the same time he sent Victor across the plain, with instructions to occupy the village of Marengo, and carefully reconnoitre the banks of the Bormida.

The First Consul fixed his headquarters at Torre di Garafolo, a considerable distance in the rear. Desaix marched off, and found no enemy. Victor pressed on to Marengo, sustained a skirmish with an Austrian outpost, and dislodged it from the village. But night was fast coming on; the staff officer entrusted with the task of reconnoitring the Bormida did not do his duty; and he returned to headquarters with the report that the enemy had no bridge on the Bormida. He was mistaken. In a deep loop of the river opposite Alessandria, they had two or three bridges.

Bonaparte was now in a strange position. He knew not really where his enemy lay. He was told, he says, that Mélas had left only a garrison in Alessandria, but where Mélas had gone he knew not, and none, apparently, could tell him. It is evident from the extended positions he assigned to his divisions that he did not know he was in presence of an enemy, and that the last thing he expected was the thing which was actually about to occur. In expectation of some correct intelligence of the movements of his adversary, he placed the divisions of Lannes and Victor in *échelon* on the old road from Tortona to Alessandria.

Gardanne was posted in Pedrabona, opposite the Austrian bridges, which he did not discover, although his left flank rested on the bank of the Bormida. Chambarlhac stood in support at Marengo, with a marsh and rivulet in front, and the river on the left flank. These two divisions formed the left wing of the army. With them, and in their rear, was Kellerman's brigade of cavalry. The next step in the *echelon* was formed by the corps of Lannes, also consisting of two divisions. It was deployed in front of San Juliano, nearly four miles in rear of Victor. One-half of the corps of Desaix, with the general, was on the march towards Novi, the other, under Monnier, bivouacked near the headquarters at Torre di Garafolo, still further in the rear. On the right, a brigade of cavalry, commanded by Rivaud, was posted on the road towards Sale, to keep a lookout on the lower Tanaro and the Po. Desaix and Rivaud were each fully seven miles from the field of battle.

This want of compactness shows that Bonaparte did not anticipate that on the morrow Mélas would throw nearly the whole of his army upon the head of the *echelon*, and strive to crush the divisions in detail. It is remarkable, however, that both generals detached largely on the 13th; and both from a similar cause. Mélas sent one-half of his fine cavalry towards Acqui, fearing that the army of Italy, under Massena and Suchet, which he knew was at Dego and Montenotte, would break in upon his rear; and Bonaparte detached Desaix towards Novi with the double object of looking out for the army of Italy, and anticipating Mélas on the road to Genoa.

But Mélas knew that he should fight a battle on the morrow in a plain most suitable for cavalry, the arm in which he far outnumbered his opponent; whereas, Bonaparte did not dream that he was about to be attacked, or we may be sure he would not have detached a man, since his practice was to call in detachments on the eve of a battle, and neglect none, however small. It is worth noting, as we shall see, that while the cavalry of Mélas rode off out of his reach, the infantry of Desaix were still within call.

The plain of Marengo was covered with cultivation, There were vineyards, and cornfields, and pastures. Enclosures abounded, and lanes intersected the fields. The great road from Tortona divided into two, after passing the defile of San Giuliano, one branch proceeding in a westerly direction, and crossing the Bormida above Marengo, the other winding to the north-west, and striking the river opposite Alessandria. From this point the road to Sale also stretched away towards the north-east, joining at the village of Castel Ceriolo, a cross-road to La Ghilina. Marengo and Castel Ceriolo were connected by a cross-road, which for some distance ran along the eastern border of a deep marsh, lying in the angle formed by the road from Marengo to Castel Ceriolo, and the road from Alessandria to Sale.

Moreover, the latter road, on starting from the Bormida, passed between that river and another marsh; and the whole tract between the Marengo road and the Bormida was in great part impracticable in consequence of the rivulets and swamps. Midway between the Bormida and the defile of San Giuliano, the plain rose with a gentle slope, and formed a plateau, overlooked by a round hill standing between San Giuliano and La Ghilina. The framework of the battlefield was the most southerly road from Tortona to Alessandria, and the road from Alessandria to Sale. It formed a quadrilateral figure of unequal sides, the western angles being. Marengo and Castel Ceriolo, and the eastern angles being San Giuliano and La Ghilina. The main conflict took place between the old road to Tortona, and the cross-road from Castel Ceriolo to La Ghilina.

Bonaparte, as we have seen, was far from expecting a battle. Satisfied from the report of the staff-officer employed to reconnoitre the Bormida, that Mélas had no bridge over that river, he had been more anxious for news from his rear and flanks, from Chabran in the Lomellina, from Rivaud at Sale, from Desaix at Rivalta, from Moncey at Milan, than from Victor at Marengo. He went to rest, feeling secure in his front, but unquiet respecting his flanks. He rose to find that the storm had lowered, and had broken in the quarter where all seemed most peaceful. Bonaparte was surprised at Marengo.

At daybreak on the 14th of June, the Austrians crossed the Bormida by the bridges which they had already built in the centre of a loop formed by the winding of the river; and filing along the road between the Bormida and a marsh that extended across the whole breadth of the base of the loop, they divided their forces into two columns where the causeway touched the firmer ground. The stronger column, both horse and foot, took ground to its right, and followed the Tortona road. The lesser column moved off to the left in order to turn the right of the French by the road to Sale. The marshes on the banks of the rivulet, whose course is parallel to the Bormida, prevented them from a direct and compact movement *en masse* into the plain.

The left column, commanded by Mélas in person, debouching from the causeway, fell upon Gardanne in the village of Pedrabona, and overpowering him by numbers and the suddenness of the attack, sent him flying towards the rear, where he rallied on the right of Chambarlhac's division, which Victor, alarmed by the storm of fire in his front, had deployed with its left on the brink of the Bormida and its right at Marengo; having Champeaux's horsemen in rear of the left.

The front of battle was nearly a mile in length and formed the head of a defile. Victor gallantly made good his ground and fought his handful of men against the bulk of the Austrian army with great obstinacy, hindering them as long as he could from breaking through and deploying on the plain. But Mélas soon extended his right and left, and sent a body of cavalry along the banks of the Bormida to turn the left flank of the French. The latter, thus vigorously assailed, could not hold their ground, and already runaways were stealing off from the flanks and rear, and spreading the alarm as far as San Giuliano. On the Austrian left, Ott, leading his column up the Sale road, had anticipated the French at Castel Ceriolo, and was already entering the plain on their right flank.

The surprise was complete. The first news of the battle which

Bonaparte received at Torre di Garafolo was the sound of the cannonade, borne thither by the morning breeze. He was astonished, but not dismayed. His first care was to send an express to Desaix, bidding him return instantly and with all speed to the plain of Marengo. Then mounting his horse he rode to San Giuliano, and saw his soldiers flying before the enemy.

To restore, or at all events to sustain the fight, and give Desaix time to rejoin the army, he sent forward Lannes from San Giuliano to take post on the right of Victor, behind the road from Marengo to Castel Ceriolo. Monnier, who had to march from Torre di Garafolo to the field of battle, and Cara St Cyr were ordered to oppose the enemy on the extreme right. The consular guard, all grenadiers, 800 strong, were sent across the plain to take post on the right of Lannes. Riding himself towards Marengo, Bonaparte hoped thus to outflank Mélas when, driving Victor before him, he deployed on the plain. But he had miscalculated the movements of the Austrians.

After defending Marengo and the banks of the rivulet with great tenacity, the corps of Victor was broken and forced to fall back in disorder on the road to Tortona. The Austrians had stormed Marengo, and were now extending their masses in the plain. Ott had defiled through Castel Ceriolo, and his foot and horse were breaking in upon Monnier, upon St. Cyr, upon the Guard. Lannes, deprived of the support of Victor on his left, and threatened by Ott on his right flank, was forced to give ground, slowly indeed, but surely. On all sides the Austrian troops came storming in, and shooting the unaccustomed cries of victory.

The left wing of the French, under Victor, was now in complete disorder, and hurrying pell-mell along the road to Tortona. Yet the bold front shown by Lannes, and the steadiness of his retreat, covered on its right by the gallant charges of Cara Si Cyr, held back the Austrians, who at this period bitterly felt the want of the cavalry, sent towards Acqui. Lannes, fighting every inch of ground, smiting the advancing infantry and horsemen, compelled his opponents to force him back by throwing forward their right upon the heels of Victor.

St Cyr, unbeaten, and obliged to retire because the troops on his left gave ground, continued to menace the left flank of the advance, and chock the rash of Ott's soldiers. The Guard, retiring in square, also resisted the Austrian cavalry, and formed a moveable redoubt in front of the interval between Lannes and St Cyr.

The Austrians, however, were steadily and decisively gaining on their foe. The fire of their guns, the hail of their bullets, the charges of their horse, and, above all, the unresisted progress of their right, forced Lannes across the plateau, with his right across the La Ghilina road, to the very foot of the hillock between that village and San Giuliano. Bonaparte, calm and unshaken, animated the drooping spirits of his soldiers by those stirring wards which he knew how to use in moments of peril as well as in moments of triumph, and, aided by Berthier—also a good man in the hour of trial—he contrived to rally the left at San Giuliano, and cover the road destined to admit the reserve under Desaix to the field of battle. Marmont also contrived to unite a few guns, and to place them in a position to batter the Austrian right, and disturb, but not stop its progress.

At this moment, when Desaix was just entering the defile of San Giuliano, Victor's shattered brigades formed the left of the French line on the left of the Tortona road; on his right were Kellerman's horsemen, and on their right the divisions of Lannes and Cara St. Cyr. The battle seemed to be lost. The Austrians believed they had won the day; eagerly advancing in pursuit, they lost their compact formation, and pressed on to complete the victory. Mélas had thrown all his men into the fight, and had no reserve. His hope now was to crush the French left, gain the road to Tortona, and cut off the French right.

His heavy columns, therefore, hastened up the road, and his flankers, driving in the small bodies opposed to them, were edging towards the Novi road. For nearly five miles, the French had been driven backwards, broken on their left, and constantly and roughly beaten in their centre. The only hope that remained to the French was in the constancy of Lannes and stern determination of Bonaparte to maintain San Giuliano.

Desaix had outstripped the march of his division, and had ridden to the side of Bonaparte. The First Consul asked him what he thought of the aspect of the battle. "It is entirely lost," answered the gallant soldier; "but it is only two o'clock, and there is time to gain another." It was true.

The Austrians, believing in victory, had spread a wide net to envelope their opponents. The columns also that were moving up the Tortona road were placed in *échelons*, great distances apart. They went forward to a pursuit and not a battle. The Hungarian infantry who led—all good soldiers—were more than half a mile from their supports. They were destined to meet a worthy foe.

Desaix's troops had at length come up, and Bonaparte placed them in columns in front of San Giuliano. On their right were the cavalry of Kellerman and Champeaux, connecting Desaix with Lannes. The crisis of the battle, the decisive movement had come. If Zach and his Hungarians were successful in defeating Desaix, the French would have been completely routed and forced to retire, as Bonaparte says he had arranged to retire by the road to Sale and the Po—a painful oblique retreat, hard to accomplish in the presence of a foe inspired by victory. It was at this moment that the most brilliant and memorable encounter in this great battle occurred.

As Zach came triumphantly up the road, Desaix led on his men, and the two columns hurled upon each other a murderous fire. Marmont's battery now came into play with great effect upon the head and left flank of the Hungarians; but they did not halt. No nation ever produced a tougher infantry than the Hungarian. Unhappily, Desaix, cheering on his men, was shot down at their head, and killed on the spot. In the midst of the uproar of the fight no one saw him fall, and the fine words put in his mouth by Bonaparte were never spoken by the heroic soldier, who died while the fight was doubtful.

The Hungarian skirmishers only had been driven back upon the main body, and Desaix's men hesitated at the aspect of their numerous and martial foes. But unexpected succour was at hand. Kellerman had kept pace on an even line with the column of Desaix. He was on the French right of the great road, partly concealed by some vineyards, and keenly watching the progress of the fight. Seizing a moment when the Hungarians were wholly occupied with the French in their front, whom they were smiting down with their fire, and were marching on with firm and steady steps, Kellerman wheeled his heavy horsemen to the left, and detaching one-half to front the Austrian cavalry flanking the Hungarian column, plunged with the other squadron, like a thunder-bolt into the left flank.

Had a bolt from Heaven fallen among them, the Hungarians could not have been more astounded. While Kellerman's horsemen were plying their sabres among them, Boudet, who had succeeded Desaix, made a fresh charge upon the head of the column. The work was done. Kellerman's happy charge—the work of a moment, a splendid instance of what a small body of sabres can do, if properly led—and Boudet's impetuous advance, seconded, as it was, by the support of Victor's rallied divisions, changed the face of the battle. The whole Hungarian column was broken and dispersed; 6,000 men laid down their arms, with Zach and his staff still at their head. The battle had been lost and won.

Kellerman pursued his career, and charged the distant *échelons* of Kaim and Haddick, and overthrew their cavalry. Lannes and St. Cyr, seeing the fire of the combat advancing on, their left, swept forward without hesitation; and thus the French line, but now broken, shattered, dispirited, thinking of retreat, was, in consequence of Kellerman's able use of the horse and the sabre, striding with the momentum of victory, forward this time, across the plain. The Austrians halted at Marengo, and made an attempt to stop the triumphant battalions. In vain.

They were attacked, overthrown, and pressed upon the narrow road that led between the marsh and the Bormida. Ott had barely time to carry the remains of his brigades through Castel Ceriolo; and the French, pursuing with that impetuosity which is their characteristic, grew more exalted in spirit as they became certain of victory. The routed foe took shelter in Alessandria, leaving behind a score of cannons, 6,000 prisoners, and heaps, of dead and dying. The French loss was not so great, but it reached, in killed, wounded, and prisoners, upwards of 4,000 men.

Who won the battle of Marengo? The popular notion is that Desaix gave the First Consul the victory. The champions of cavalry, as an all-conquering arm, claim it for Kellerman, and Kellerman loudly claimed it for himself. On the other hand, while admitting that Kellerman's charge was the happiest incident in the battle, the champions of Bonaparte claim for him the credit of Kellerman's charge. In our estimation, the glory gathered on the field of Marengo cannot be monopolized by any one name. The stern courage and admirable constancy of Lannes were conspicuous, and, had he not displayed those qualities, Desaix's division would never have arrived at the defile of San Giuliano.

And if Desaix came to the ground in time, we must not forget that it was Bonaparte who called him. Kellerman's charge, too, Savary says, was not the inspiration of a moment. It was made by the express orders of Bonaparte, who sent the order by Savary himself. The name of Desaix will ever be associated with the name of Marengo; for three reasons; because he died upon the field; because he counselled hope when he might have counselled despair; and because he charged the enemy like one certain to win, instead of using his troops with uncertain resolution, to cover a retreat Marengo was won by Bonaparte's unshaken resolution and inimitable skill, by the hardihood of Desaix; by the quickness and energy of Kellerman; by Victor, courageous, though unfortunate; and by Lannes, firm and invincible, though forced to give ground.

Marmont also, and his artillerymen, must have some share of the renown of this stoutly-contested and suddenly-conquered field. It is not just to heap upon one brow all the laurels gathered in a victorious battle. The master of war who designed those combinations which united his battalions and squadrons on the banks of the Bormida, in the very field he had selected three months before, as the point of collision with the enemy whom he had outwitted, has acquired so much glory from the execution of this splendid design, that his friends and adulators may spare a few bright rays for the brows of his able generals.

Nor should the vanquished be deprived of their share of honour. No soldiers could have fought better. But Mélas, who had won the victory in the early afternoon, can never be pardoned for allowing it to slip from his grasp in the evening,

Mélas gave up the struggle with Bonaparte, accepting his defeat at Marengo as decisive of the campaign. He had still an army almost as numerous as that of his enemy, but he was enclosed in a net; and, although by great good luck and able generalship he might have escaped, he did not think it prudent to try. The very morning after the battle he sent a flag of truce to the camp of the victor to arrange the terms of a convention.

Bonaparte was not inclined to create difficulties, and the business was soon concluded. It was at once arranged that the Austrians should retire behind the Mincio, on condition that they gave up Savona, Ceva, Genoa, Coni, Alessandria, Tortona, Milan, Turin, Pizzighettone, Piacenza, and Arona, within a specified time. All the Austrian cannon in these fortresses were to belong to the Austrian army, all other cannon to the French. The provisions were to be equally divided. The Austrians were to occupy the country behind the Mincio, Borgoforte on the Po, Ferrara in the Legations, Ancona in the Romagna, and Tuscany. The French army were to have their front positions on the Chiese and the Oglio; and a tract of country between the two armies was to be neutral ground. Neither army was to attack the other without ten days' notice, should either side resolve to put an end to the armistice.

Thus a daring march and a great battle restored Lombardy and Piedmont to the French, and the fruits of the victories of Mélas and Suwarrof in 1799 were recaptured at one blow. Nothing remained to the Austrians but Mantua, and a precarious position south of the Po.

Bonaparte returned once more to Milan. His object now was

to establish the power of France in Lombardy, Piedmont, and Liguria, on strong foundations; to give an air of independence to the Italian Governments, but to make them subservient in reality to the military pro-consuls he was about to leave behind. The army, base of all power in this system, was reorganized; and Massena, called to Milan, and appointed to command it, became for the time being, under Bonaparte, master of the destinies of the Italians.

Bonaparte desired to efface the memories of his exactions and of the plunder of his soldiers in 1796-7; and, being now practically supreme, he gave a more regular form to the Government, but he did not the less remain the lord of these liberated people. In his relations with Massena he already played the part of master, feeling that he really was so.

On the 25th of June he set out from Milan for Paris, passing through Turin, over Mont Cénis, by Lyons, Dijon, and Sens, worshipped at every town he entered by a race always greedy of military glory, and always ready to draw the chariot of a conqueror. Bonaparte had quitted Paris on the 6th of May to carry his Army of Reserve over the Alps into the heart of sunny Italy. On the night of the 2nd of July he re-entered the capital of France; having in the interval of fifty-seven days performed such notable exploits, and won back those splendid provinces which the Directory had lost.

Here end the Italian Campaigns of General Bonaparte, for in Italy, Bonaparte, soon to become Napoleon I., warred no more.

The war, however, did not then terminate, France and Austria could not agree upon the terms of peace, and Austria held out for six months longer, out of deference to England, rather than make a separate treaty. During this period, Bonaparte's generals in Germany, in Italy, in the Valteline, and the Tyrol conducted some brilliant campaigns; of which the more remarkable were Macdonald's winter campaign in the wild and rugged valleys that lie between the sources of the Ticino and the valley of the Adda, and Moreau's German campaign, which was terminated by the victory at Hohenlinden. Austria was constrained to sign

the treaty of Lunéville in February, 1801; and Consul Bonaparte thereby exacted again, with some additions, those advanta-
geous terms, which General Bonaparte had, in 1797, insisted on
at Campo-Formio

CHAPTER 4 [1]

1859

The French are once more the invaders of Italy, and another Bonaparte leads a second crusade for the "liberation" of that beautiful land from the grasp of the hateful "stranger." Again, a French ruler strikes a blow at the house of Austria on the Ticino, the Po, the Mincio, and the Adige. Again, victory has crowned the first onset of the French legions, and a Passage of the Ticino has rivalled the Passage of the Apennines. Deeming that a comparison of the different circumstances under which the two invasions have been made will not be unacceptable, this chapter is appended as a memorandum in the hope that it may prove useful to curious readers.

The first thing that strikes the observer is that the Napoleon of our day has Piedmont for an ally, and not for an enemy. Next, that he has started, not from Liguria, but from Alessandria and the Po. Thirdly, that he has not had to depend at first upon limited and precarious communications, traversing barren rocks and dangerous shores, but that he has had open to him all the roads into Italy, including the silent highway of the sea; and that he has been able to transport men, materiel, and stores, to Genoa and to Leghorn, and to send a fleet of war ships into the Adriatic, as well as to march his battalions over the Mont Cénis. Fourthly, one great fact must be noted; the contending armies are four times as great as they were in 1796, and more than three as great

---

1. For some of the details in this chapter the author is greatly indebted to an admirable article in the *Revue des Deux Mondes* for the 1st April, 1859.

as they were in 1800.

Nor is this all: new arms have been invented, rifled cannon and rifled muskets; new appliances, the electric telegraph used in the field, the apparatus of the photographer, above all the railway and the steamship, which have vastly augmented the locomotive power of armies, lessened their fatigues, and brought them with speed and freshness to the very verge of the field of battle. These are great and important differences. It is true that the balance in favour of our day over the days of old is shared by both sides, though in an unequal degree, for the Austrians have no commanding marine.

In 1796, the people, especially those of Piedmont and the States of Venice were animated by a strong dislike of the French. In 1859 there is hardly an Italian, except he be a priest, or a noble highly placed in the service of Austria, or an ignorant peasant besotted with superstition, who is not devoted to France; because the French chief of 1859, like his predecessor of 1796, is regarded as the "liberator" of Italy. In order to link the two epochs, and in some measure contrast them, take the following manifesto from the French *Moniteur* of June 11, 1859:—

The fortune of war has conducted me to the capital of Lombardy. Let me tell you why I am here.

When Austria unjustly attacked Piedmont, I resolved to sustain the King of Sardinia, my ally. The honour and interests of France made this my duty.

Your enemies, who are my enemies, have endeavoured to diminish the sympathy which exists throughout all Europe for your cause, by trying to persuade the world that I am carrying on this war only for personal ambition, or to aggrandise the territory of France.

If there are men who do not understand their epoch, I am not of the number.

In the enlightened state of public opinion which prevails, men are greater by the moral influence which they exercise than by barren conquests, and this moral influence I seek after with pride in contributing to emancipate one of the most beautiful parts of Europe.

Your reception has already proved to me that you have understood me. I do not come here with any preconceived plan to dispossess sovereigns, nor to impose my own will upon you. My army will only occupy itself with two things:—To combat your enemies, and to maintain internal order. It will place no obstacle in the way of a free manifestation of your legitimate wishes.

Providence sometimes favours nations like individuals in giving them occasion to rise suddenly to greatness; but it is on condition that they have the virtue to profit by it. Profit then by the fortune which is offered you. Your desire of independence, so long expressed, so often deceived, will be realised if you show yourselves worthy of it.

Unite then for one sole object, the enfranchisement of your country. Seek military organisation. Hasten all of you to place yourselves under the flag of King Victor Emmanuel, who has already so nobly shown you the path of honour. Remember that without discipline there is no army, and animated with the sacred fire of patriotism be nothing today but soldiers. Tomorrow you will be free citizens of a great country.

Done at the Imperial quarters, at Milan, the 8th of June 1859.

Napoleon.

But while there has been change in those things to which we have referred, and while the political geography of the country has altered—Venice and Genoa, which existed as independent States in 1796, having long been buried in history in the graves dug for them by Napoleon Bonaparte and the Congress of Vienna—yet the great physical features of the land, the rivers, the swamps, the lakes, the mountains, remain what they were sixty-three years ago. These do not change, or change so slightly that they do not affect the strategy of war.

It has been seen that in our day the French invading army has had free access to the plains of Piedmont by the Alps, the sea, and the Apennines. In crossing the Mont Cénis the infantry were reminded of the genius of Napoleon the First; and the horsemen who lately rode along the Corniche to the gates of friendly Genoa, must also have remembered who it was that opened this fine road. On their side, also, the Austrians have made roads that did not exist in 1796. There is the great railway which links Vienna with Verona, Mantua, and Milan. In addition to the mountain road through the Tyrol that, climbing the Brenner, passes by Trent and down the valley of the Adige, they have made another road into the valley of the Adige by the valley of the Drave.

They have also connected the valley of the Adige and the valley of the Upper Adda by a new road, carried over the lofty ridge of the Stelvio into the Valteline. This road, constructed in part above the limits of the eternal snows, is a marvellous work of engineering. It traverses ravines on bridges, it dives under hills, and descends in steep gradients abrupt precipices. It is regarded as a strong line of military communication with Como and Milan, because it may be easily defended; but it may be questioned whether, with an insurrection in the Valteline, it would be of great service in a campaign beyond securing a line of retreat, easily closed to a pursuing force, or in serving as a route along which a corps might be sent to vex and threaten the rear of an army fronting the Mincio.

Then there is a road over the Mont Tonale which connects one of the affluents of the Adige with head waters of the Oglio, and joins the great Lombard highway between Milan and Brescia. The road over the lofty Tonale is connected with a road extending westward to the basin of the little lake, Lake Idro, and passing down the eastern shore of the lake into the rugged and dangerous defile of the Val Sabbia, and connecting it with the base of the Lake of Garda. All these roads have been made for the purpose of giving Austrian troops a flank access into the plains of Lombardy. They may be turned against her by a daring chief, who with a sufficient force should carry on a partisan war in the hills and deep glens so suitable for that kind of fighting, because they give access to the Tyrol and the flank of the Austrian line of communication by the valley of the Adige, as well as access to Lombardy.

The Austrians have farther increased the facilities for entering Lombardy by constructing a railway from Verona up the valley of the Adige as far as Botzen. This places them in direct communication with the immense fortress which they have constructed at Brixen, covering the roads to the Brenner Pass on one side, and the valley of the Drave on the other. Joubert, in 1797, marched through Brixen on his way to join Bonaparte in Styria, a feat he could not have performed had the stronghold of Brixen then existed. Further to the east, the valley of the Brenta has been connected with the valley of the Piave by Feltre and Belluno, and the road has been continued up the Piave and over the Col de Toblach into the valley of the Drave. Such are the main lines of communication, far more complete than those of 1796, between Lombardo-Venetia and Germany, the greatest and most important being the Lombardo-Venetian Railway and the line from Verona to Botzen.

Then there are the means of defence in Lombardo-Venetia. These have greatly changed since 1796. The plain of Lombardy lies between the Po and the great mountain chains that rise on the frontiers of France and stretch away as far as the frontiers of Germany. In its broadest part this basin is not more than sixty miles across; in its narrowest not more than thirty. The mountains, which rise like walls in the west and recede a little from the plain, press forward in bold and elevated spurs towards the east, and project forward, where the Adige enters the plain, like a huge bastion, contracting the interval between their bases and the Po.

In these mountains many torrents rise, which, gathering up the waters of affluents plenteously fed by the snows, flow down to augment the volume of the Po. All these streams run transversely across Lombardy. The Ticino, separating Piedmont from Lombardy, rises in the St Gothard and the Splugen, and feeds, with other streams, the Lago Maggiore. Issuing from the southern extremity of that beautiful lake, it flows through a fertile country, broad, deep, and rapid, until it falls into the Po, a little below Pavia. This frontier river is not defensible, on account of its great length. But in order to prevent an enemy from repeating the manoeuvre of Bonaparte in 1796, and turning the line from Alessandria and Genoa, and in order to control the populations on the southern bank of the Po, the Austrians constructed the famous entrenched camp of Piacenza, which on the 4th of June, 1859, Napoleon the Third rendered useless by passing the Ticino at Turbigo and Buffalora. Piacenza and its entrenched camp were again fatal to the Austrians; and a stronghold which military men were disposed to think would play a considerable part in the campaign, overestimated as to its importance by the Austrians, only proved a snare.

From the Ticino to the Mincio there are many streams and two important rivers: the Adda, rising far up in the Valteline, coursing along that mountain valley, flowing through the Lake of Como, and winding its way from the lake across Lombardy to the Po, a few miles west of Cremona; and the Oglio, which, fed by the ice-covered summits of the Mont Tonale, rushes down the Val Canonica, traverses Lake Iseo, and flows in a bold curve through the plain to the Po. On the Adda are Lodi and Pizzighettone—the latter a strong place, but small.

The Oglio receives several affluents, of which the Mélas, coming from the Val Trompia, and the Chiese from the Val Sabbia and Lake Idro are the most important. Neither of these rivers offer a good line of defence. Both are long and convex towards an enemy, thus affording great facilities for an attacking force to move upon the upper part of the stream, if the lower be defended, or, Piacenza being taken or abandoned, the line of both may be turned by a force following the right bank of the Po, and crossing below the points of confluence.

These considerations will explain the rapid retreat of Beaulieu in 1796, and of Gyulai and Hess in 1859. In one case Bonaparte turned the Austrian position and nearly seized their line of retreat by passing the Po at Piacenza in rear of Beaulieu, who was on the left bank of the Po and the left bank of the Ticino. In the other, Napoleon the Third and Victor Emmanuel, reversing the process, deceived his enemy at Piacenza and crossed the Ticino forty miles above its confluence with the Po.

The bulwark of the Austrian possessions in Italy is the quadrangle between the Mincio and the Adige; and it is here that the Austrian engineers and strategists have lavished all the resources of their art. The Mincio, like the other principal rivers of this part of Italy, flows through a lake. Rising on the southern slopes of Mount Tonale, where it is called the Sarca, it enters the Lake of Garda, and issuing thence at Peschiera, flows by Mantua into the Po.

It is rapid, but not deep. It is fordable in many places, as we have seen, and it is crossed by several stone bridges. The Adige springs in the mountains of the Tyrol, follows a course parallel to that of the Mincio, which it approaches near Verona, and loses itself below Legnago in the lagunes and marshes of the Po. The Adige is not fordable in any part; it is broad, deep, and rapid. As a line of defence it is more favourable than any other.

At the angles of the quadrangle lying between these rivers are four strong places. The Mincio is flanked by Peschiera on its right, and on its left, five-and-twenty miles distant, stands Mantua. The Adige, in like manner, is flanked by Verona on its right, opposite to Peschiera, and distant from it a dozen miles, and by Legnago on its left, distant from Mantua five-and-thirty miles in a direct line. Each fortress is very strong.

Peschiera stands in an island formed by the Mincio as it leaves the Lake of Garda. On the left bank of the Mincio, three lunettes, constructed on a hillock overlooking that side, form its external defence. On the right bank, eight bomb-proof lunettes crown a slight rise in the ground and form the outworks of an entrenched camp. Yet Peschiera is supposed to be the weakest of the fortresses, because the capture of one of the western redoubts involves the capture of all. The advantage which the Austrians hope to obtain by Peschiera is that its garrison would threaten the flank of a force attempting to cross the Mincio, where Bonaparte crossed it, at Borghetto.

There is a flotilla on the Lake of Garda and a system of sluices connected with the fortress, by opening which the volume of water in the Mincio can be augmented. It will be seen that these fortifications are far stronger, or at least more extensive, than those of Peschiera in 1796. Besides, at that time, Peschiera and the whole country belonged to Venice, an obstacle in the path of both armies, and regarded by Austria more than by France.

Mantua, so far as we can learn, is pretty much in the same state as it was when Bonaparte reduced it by famine. It stands on three islands formed by the Mincio, which assumes the dimensions of a lake more than a mile across. The country all around is marshy, and the air laden with fever and ague. There are five raised causeways connecting the firm land with the islands, and four forts defend these narrow ways: the citadel and St George's on the east, and the Pictole (added by Napoleon) and the Pradella on the west.

The islands are large enough to contain a small army. But Mantua, although so strong as to be deemed impregnable, can, as we have seen, be easily blockaded by posting bodies of troops at the heads of the causeways. The source of its strength for defence is the source of its weakness for offence; and except as a place which may be held long enough to cause great disquietude, trouble and even danger to an army directed against the Adige, and as a fort which, so long as it holds out, gives Austria a grip of Italy, Mantua does not seem likely to play any other part in the campaign of 1859. How long it will be defended depends upon the state of its magazines and the moral courage of its governor. In 1796, under an Austrian, it held out for six months; in 1799, under a Frenchman, it surrendered in three.

Verona is now the most formidable fortress in North Italy. It stands upon the Adige at the mouth of the gorges of the Tyrol, where the river breaks through the spurs of the mountain chain, in a country of gardens and vineyards, broken and difficult. Here are the headquarters of the Italian army, and the central depôt for all belligerent wants of that army. The old walls, erected by

Italian engineers, have been strengthened by new defences, and two strong forts protect, the one the entrance, the other the issue of the river.

Connected with the fortress is a vast entrenched camp on the right bank of the Adige. The Austrian engineers have taken advantage of an extensive depression of the soil, and have built redoubts upon the encircling ridges, six hundred or seven hundred yards apart; thus forming a rallying place for a whole army. The defences on the left bank are less imposing, but still formidable. The possession of Verona gives the Austrians, as it gave Bonaparte, the command of both banks of the Adige. Close to Peschiera, and connected therewith, the army in Verona can give it succour if attacked, and can assail or menace any force attempting to pass between the Lake of Garda and the Adige.

The fourth fortress, Legnago, is a small town on the Adige, seated on its left bank, and having a double bridge-head, giving access to either side of the stream. It is connected with Verona by a road purposely carried between a canal and the Adige, to give it greater security. Napoleon recognised the importance of Legnago, and directed certain improvements in its defences, which have been made.

The reader will now see that the country between the Mincio and the Adige presents an obstacle to an invader incomparably more difficult to overcome than the same country in 1796. Bonaparte rapidly blockaded Mantua, passed the Mincio, and seized Peschiera; and in his defensive campaigns he made.

Verona the pivot of all his operations. Now, the passage of the Mincio and the sieges of Peschiera and Mantua promise to be only the first acts in the drama. The loss of either will still leave the line of the Adige and the Austrian communications intact, and Verona and the Adige must be taken ere the Austrians are pushed into or from the mountains. Whether these formidable defences can be made good will depend as much upon Austrian generalship and Austrian morale as upon the rivers and swamps and strongholds.

In addition to these changes made by time and war in Upper Italy, there is one other of great importance. Bonaparte destroyed the old Republic of Venice, and gave her and the States she owned on *terra firma* to the Austrian. In this war Venice promises to be another strong weapon of defence. Seated in her lagoons, she is supposed to be unassailable from the sea. If captured, the fort of Malaghera, standing in the midst of a marsh, and absolutely commanding the road from the firm land into Venice, would still have to be taken.

But if Venice were to succumb to the fire of the new rifled cannon, and the Malaghera were captured, or if a French force could manage to land on the marshy shores of the Adriatic between Venice and Trieste, the line of the Adige would be taken in reverse, and the enemy would hold the direct line of communication with Vienna. This shows the immense advantages, beside those already enumerated, that may result . from the command of the sea, advantages of which the fleets of England deprived Bonaparte in 1796.

Yet the advantages on the side of Austria are enormous, and if she cannot defend her possessions by the aid of such advantages, it will be evident that her days as the great central balance-weight of Europe will have come to an end.

Appendix

Many of the despatches in the Napoleon Correspondence, published by the order of the present Emperor have been placed already before the public in different works; but it may not be inappropriate at this moment to lay before the reader some extracts showing to a certain extent, how Bonaparte, acting for France, and always with a view to augment the power of France, and thereby to increase his own, conducted himself towards the people and the states of Italy.

Let us begin with a passage from a despatch to the Directory, dated from Milan, May 17, 1796,

> The tricolour flag floats over Milan, Pavia, Como, and all the cities of Lombardy. . . . . The Austrian army is beyond the Mincio. It has already received a reinforcement of 6,000 men. It is expecting 10,000 more, who are on the road. This will only increase the glory of the armies of the Republic. Milan is very much inclined to liberty. There is a club of 800 individuals, all lawyers or merchants. We are going to leave in existence the forms of government which are in usage. We shall only change the persons who, having been named by Ferdinand (Emperor of Germany), cannot merit our confidence. We shall get out of this country a contribution of 20,000,000. This country is one of the richest in the universe, but entirely exhausted by five years of war from this place will be issued the newspapers, and writings of all kinds which will set Italy in a blaze, where the alarm is extreme.

If these people want to be organised into a republic, is it to be granted to them? That is a question which is for you to decide, and upon which it would be well for you to manifest your intentions. This country is much more patriotic than Piedmont. It is nearer to liberty.

We may add here a string of interesting proclamations, which serve to show the promises held out to the people of Italy, in order to win them over to the side of France.

To the Municipality of Milan.

Headquarters, Verona, 9th August, 1796.

When the army was in retreat, and the partisans of Austria and the enemies of liberty believed it lost—when it was impossible for you to suspect that this retreat was only a *ruse,* you showed attachment to France and the love of liberty. You displayed a zeal and a character which deserved the esteem of the army, and which will secure the protection of the French Republic.

Every day your people render themselves more worthy of liberty. They increase in energy every day. They will, doubtless, appear one day with glory in the theatre of the world. Accept the testimony of my satisfaction and of the sincere desire of the French people to see you free and happy.

Bonaparte.

To the Inhabitants of Reggio.

Headquarters, Milan, 7th October, 1796.

I have seen with the most lively interest, brave inhabitants of Reggio, your energy and your bravery. You have thrown yourselves into the career of liberty with a courage and a decision which will be rewarded with success. At your very first step, you gained an essential advantage, and some of your citizens have sealed with their blood the liberty of their country. Courage, brave inhabitants of Reggio; form your battalions, organize yourselves, take arms! It is time that Italy also should be counted amongst the free and powerful nations. Set the example, and merit the gratitude of posterity.

Bonaparte.

To the People of Bologna.

Bologna, 19th October, 1796.

On my entrance into your city, I was pleased to see the enthusiasm which animates you, and your firm resolution to preserve your liberty. The constitution of your National Guard shall soon be organized; but I have been afflicted to see certain excesses committed by some bad persons unworthy to be Bolognese. A people that commits excesses is unworthy of liberty. A free people is one that respects persons and property. Anarchy produces intestine wars and all sorts of public calamities.

I am the enemy of tyrants, but, above all, the sworn enemy of rascals, thieves, and anarchists. I shoot my soldiers when they steal. I shall shoot those who, reversing social order, are born for the opprobrium and misfortune of the world.

People of Bologna, do you desire that the French Republic should protect you? Do you wish the French army to esteem you, and to feel honoured by having caused your happiness? Do you wish that I should boast sometimes of the friendship which you manifest towards me? Put down this small number of rascals. Do not let anyone be oppressed, whatever may be his opinions. No one can be arrested, except according to law. Above all things, let property be respected. I am about to shoot one of the thieves. A similar fate awaits all who act as he did.

Bonaparte.

To the Congress of the State of Lombardy.

Milan, 10th December, 1796.

Citizens, I do not see anything improper in your sending deputies to the federation of Reggio. The union of patriots causes their strength. I am very glad to take this opportunity of destroying some reports which have been spread by malevolence. If Italy wishes to be free, who hereafter can hinder her? It is not enough that the different States unite. It is, above all, necessary to draw closer the bonds of fraternity between the different classes of the State. Put down, especially, the small number of men who only love liberty to get at a revolution.

They are its greatest enemies. They take all kinds of disguises to accomplish their criminal designs. The French army will never suffer liberty in Italy to be covered with crimes. You ought to be free without revolutions, without running the risks and experiencing the misfortunes which the French people have gone through. Protect property and persons; inspire in your countrymen the love of order and of the laws, and of those warlike virtues which defend and protect republics and liberty. The scene in which several riotous and bad people have got up against citizen Greppi, has created alarm and inspired a terror that you ought to try to dissipate. Put down malevolent persons, and do not allow a small number to mislead the people, and commit crimes in its name.

Bonaparte.

To the President of the Cispadane Congress.
(Extract.)

. . . . Poor Italy has for some time disappeared from the list of European powers. If the Italians of the present day are worthy to recover their rights, and to give themselves a free Government, we shall one day see their country figure gloriously among the powers of the globe. But do not forget that laws are nothing without force. Your first glance should be directed to your military organization. Nature has given you everything; and after the unity and the wisdom that have been remarked in your different deliberations, you want nothing to attain your end, but to have veteran battalions animated by the sacred fire of patriotism.

In one of his manifestoes to the people of Romagna, Bonaparte says—

"The Commander-in-Chief repeats to the people of this beautiful country what he has said to its deputies, that, it is *neither the ambition of an extension of territory, nor the lust of conquest,* which has brought the French army among them; but the necessity of chasing from the Court of Rome the enemies of the French Republic; and the General takes the opportunity of improving as much as he can, the civil, political, and economical government of this fine country, which has for so long a time been subjected to absolute government in a form so afflicting to humanity."

"There are at this moment," he writes, on the 28th of December, 1796, "three parties in Lombardy: first, those who allow themselves to be led by the French; secondly, those who wish for liberty and even show their desire with some impatience; thirdly, those who are friends of the Austrians and enemies of the French. I sustain and encourage the first, control the second, and repress the third. . . . .The Cispadane Republics are also divided into three parties: first, the friends of their old Government; secondly, the partisans of an independent constitution, but slightly aristocratic; thirdly, the partisans of a French constitution, or a pure democracy.

"I compress the first, sustain the second, and moderate the third. I sustain the second and moderate the third, because the second party is that of the rich proprietors and priests, who in the end will gain the mass of the people, which it is essential should rally round the French party. The third party is composed of young fellows, writers, and men, who, as in France and every country, do not change with the change of Government, and only love liberty that they may make a revolution."

"The Lombards," he writes in March, 1797, "are very impatient: they desire that their liberty should be declared, and that they should be also permitted to make a constitution."

A paragraph from one of Bonaparte's manifestoes, copied in a mutilated form from the *Moniteur Universel,* of the 10th May, 1797, into the "Correspondence," addressed to the General Administration of Lombardy, is well worthy of note.

"You demand," he says, "assurances for your future independence, but these assurances, do they not exist in, the victories won every day by the army of Italy? . . . Every one of our victories is a line in your constitutional charter. . . . Facts fill the place of a declaration, puerile by itself. . . . You cannot doubt the interest and strongly expressed desire of the Government to make you free and independent," &c.

Bonaparte's treatment of Venice is a remarkable illustration of his policy. At first he professed friendship, and appealed to Venice as an ally.

To the Republic of Venice.
Head Quarters, Brescia, 29th May, 1796.
It was to deliver the finest country of Europe from the iron yoke of the proud house of Austria that the French army brayed obstacles the most difficult to surmount. Victory, in accordance with justice, crowned its efforts. The remains of the enemy's army have retired beyond the Mincio. The French army, in pursuing them, passes over the territory of the Republic of Venice, but it will not forget that a long friendship unites these two republics. Religion, Government, customs, property, will be respected.
Let the people be free from alarm. The severest discipline will be maintained. All that is furnished to the army will be strictly paid for in money. The Commander-in-Chief begs the officers of the Venetian Republic, the magistrates,

and the priests, to make known his sentiments to the people, in order that perfect trust may cement the friendship which has long united the two nations. Faithful in the path of honour as in that of victory, the French soldier is only terrible to the enemies of his liberty and his Government.

Bonaparte.

"The Senate of Venice," he writes on the 7th June, 1796, "has sent me two Sages of the Council to give them definite information concerning the state of things. I renewed my complaints to them. I also spoke to them of the reception given to *Monsieur*; I told them that I had rendered you an account of everything, and that I did not know how you would take it; that when I left Paris. you believed we should find in the Republic of Venice an ally faithful to its principles; that it was only with regret I had been compelled to think otherwise by their conduct with regard to Peschiera; that, however, I believed it was a storm that it would be possible for the *envoyé* of the Senate to disperse. In the meantime, they lend themselves with the best grace to supplying us with what is necessary for the army.

"If your project is to get five or six millions out of Venice, this little rupture which I have purposely contrived will suit your purpose; and you can ask them as indemnity for the combat at Borghetto, which I was obliged to fight in order to take the place. If you have stronger intentions, I think you must continue this subject of quarrel, instructing me as to what you want to have done, and waiting the favourable moment, which I will seize according to circumstances; for we must not be involved with everyone at the same time.

"The truth of the affair at Peschiera is this—Beaulieu deceived them in a dastardly way; he asked for the passage of fifty men, and he took possession of the city."

After much bickering, many explosions of wrath, and an extremely able handling of the Venetians, against whom he had long nursed a quarrel, he wrote thus, on the 24th of March, 1797, giving an account of an interview with Pesaro, who had been sent to his headquarters at Goritz to propitiate the conqueror of the Archduke Charles:—

"I told M. Pesaro," he says, "that the Executive Directory did not forget that the Republic of Venice was an ancient ally of France; that we have a strong desire to protect Venice from every other Power; and I only asked that bloodshed should cease, and that those citizens should not be considered criminal who had more inclination for the French than for the imperial army; that we did not sustain the insurgents [*they were commanded by Landrieux, a French officer*]; and that, on the contrary, we favoured the measures of the Government; but that, as I believed the Venetian Government had sent a courier to the Directory, it would be best, perhaps, to wait his return, because I believed that the intervention of France would alone, and, without having recourse to arms, restore tranquillity. We quitted each other good friends; and Pesaro seemed to be well satisfied. *The great point in all this is to gain time.* I beg that you will send detailed instructions to guide my conduct"

On his return from Germany, Bonaparte, as we have seen, destroyed the Republic; and Mignet, speaking of its partition, condemns the Directory for what he calls a crime against liberty, really committed by Bonaparte.

"In the fanaticism of a system," he adds, "we may desire to set a country free, but we should never give it away. By arbitrarily distributing the territory of a small State, the Directory (*i. e.* Bonaparte) set the example of this traffic in nations, since but too much followed. Besides, the Austrian dominion would sooner or later extend in Italy, through this imprudent cession of Venice."

The intriguing policy pursued towards Venice was also pur-

sued towards the Pope, whom Bonaparte found extremely difficult to manage. He wanted to preserve a hold upon the Court of
Rome, whose value as a political agent he distinctly perceived.
A few extracts will show his double-dealing. To Cardinal Mattei
he wrote, on the 21st October, 1796:—

> The Court of Borne has refused the conditions of peace
> offered by the Directory; she has broken the armistice by
> suspending the execution of its conditions. She arms; she
> desires war; she shall have it. But, before I can look for-
> ward, in cold blood, to the ruin and death of the madmen
> who would throw obstacles in the way of the Republican
> phalanxes, I owe it to my nation, to humanity, to myself, to
> try a last effort to bring back the Pope to more moderate
> sentiments, conformable to his true interests, to his sacred
> character, to reason. You know, Cardinal, the strength and
> the power of the army I command: to destroy the tempo-
> ral power of the Pope, I have only to will it. Go to Rome;
> see the Holy Father; enlighten him on his true interests;
> snatch him from the intrigues of those who desire his ruin
> as well as that of the Court of Rome. The French Govern-
> ment permits me once more to open negotiations: all may
> be arranged.

And a few days later, namely, on the 24th October, 1796, he
sent this letter to M. Cacault, the French agent at Rome:—

> Keep me exactly informed of all you do, in order that I
> may seize the most convenient moment to execute the
> intentions of the Directory. You know that, after the peace
> with Naples and Genoa, our harmonious relations with
> the King of Sardinia, the recapture of Corsica, and our
> superiority in the Mediterranean, I only wait a favourable
> moment to throw myself on Rome, and revenge the na-
> tional honour. The great thing is to gain time. My inten-
> tion is, when I enter the States of the Pope—rather far off
> at present—to enter by virtue of the armistice, and take
> possession of Ancona. From that place it will be easier

for me to go farther, after taking good care of my rear. In short, the great art, at this time, is to throw each other the ball reciprocally, in order that we may deceive the old fox.

Four days later Bonaparte thus flung the ball to Cacault in obedience to the instructions of the Directory; but we may be sure the Directory did not hint to him that exquisite piece of hypocrisy, about being the saviour rather than destroyer of the Holy Chair.

Desiring to give the Pope a mark of my anxiety to terminate this long war, and put an end to Its misfortunes, I offer him a means of saying his honour. You can assure him that I have been always opposed to the treaty offered, and to the manner of negotiating it; and that it is in consequence of my repeated and special appeals that the Directory charged me to open a new road to negotiations. I am more ambitious of the title of saviour than that of destroyer of the Holy Chair. You know yourself that we have always had like principles thereon; and by means of the unlimited power given me by the Directory, if they will be wise at Borne, we shall profit by it to give peace to this lovely part of the world, and to quiet the timid consciences of many people.

The reader has seen that when the game of throwing the ball had been carried on long enough, Bonaparte executed the design he hinted at in his letter to Cacault on the 24th October.

Bonaparte did not take a favourable view of proposals for a congress. He much preferred to make separate treaties, and isolate his foes. On the 6th of March, 1797, just as he was about to commence his inroad into Germany, he wrote to the Directory that they could not begin a negotiation for a separate peace, and at the same time listen to any proposal for the opening of a congress:

So long as the Court of Vienna has the hope of being able

to obtain our consent to the opening of a congress, she will never hear of propositions for a separate peace. We shall never get the Court of Vienna to enter into negotiations unless we decidedly pronounce against the opening of a congress, which by the slowness of its forms could not evade the campaign about to open, and which a spirit of humanity and philosophy, unfortunately not shared by the Emperor, makes you desire to evade.

An Italian view of the French invasion will carry the reader beyond the Bonapartist into the Napoleonic period.

Bonaparte, on his return from Egypt, landed at Fréjus, on the 9th of October; he overthrew the Directory, and established the Consular Government on the 9th of November (*18th Brumaire*); sole and absolute master of France at the opening of spring, in 1800, he assembled his hosts at the foot of the Alps, achieved the passage of the Great St. Bernard May 20), and obtained a decisive victory at Marengo June 14). This, and the splendid campaign of Moreau, north of the Alps, and his triumph at Hohenlinden, bowed Austria to the peace of Lunéville (1801, February 9th), which brought Italy back to the conditions of the previous treaty of Campo Formio.
Naples and Rome, however, contrived to make their private peace with the conqueror, and the house of Parma was called to reign in 'Etruria,' or Tuscany. The Cisalpine Republic now gloried in the name of 'Italian;' and when France had raised her First Consul to the imperial dignity, in 1804, the Italian Republic was also erected into a kingdom under the same ruler, in 1805. A new outbreak of hostilities in this same year led to the further humiliation of Austria at Austerlitz, and to the peace of Pressburg (December 26), by which Venice was at last withdrawn from the Austrian yoke and united to the Kingdom of Italy.
In the following year Naples was again lost to the Bourbons, and given to Joseph Bonaparte (1806), and then

173

to Murat (1809). Before this latter year, the kingdom of Etruria, and what remained of the Papal States had been united to France. Parma and Genoa had submitted to the same fate at a previous epoch.

The future of Piedmont was for a long time left undecided. Upon the departure of the King, in 1798, Joubert had appointed a provisional regency of fifteen democrats, whose number rose afterwards to twenty-five. The country remains a nameless, nondescript republic, though it was divided into four departments (Eridano, Sesia, Stura, and Tanaro), in the French style, till it fell into the hands of the Austro-Russians, in 1799. A conqueror at Marengo, Bonaparte had for some time contemplated a restoration of the dynasty of Savoy, and had even some communication on the subject with Charles Emanuel, who lived at this time at Florence.

The King, at first, refused to treat without the knowledge and consent of his allies; he then repented, and sent the Count of St. Marsano to Paris to open negotiations, but it was already too late. Austria was brought to extremities, and the First Consul perceived that all Italy was now at his discretion. Piedmont remained in a provisional state, nevertheless, and only a committee of seven persons was appointed to govern in the name of the French Republic Later in the same year (4th October, 1800), General Jourdan was Minister Extraordinary in Piedmont, and a government commission of seven persons, and an executive board of five, were nominated by him.

Only on the 11th September, 1802, Piedmont, in six departments—Po, Dora, Sesia, Marengo, Stura, and Tanaro—became formally and definitely an integral part of the French territory. General Menou was now substituted for Jourdan. Long before this epoch, however (September and October, 1800), the provinces of Novara, Arona, Val Sesia, Ossole, Vigevano, and Lomellina, had been detached from the Piedmontese territory, and united to Milan as a part of the Cisalpine or Italian Republic. In the same manner Tortona, Voghera, Bobbio, and even Ceva and Acqui, were incorporated with the several departments of the Ligurian territory.

When the entire peninsula came at last into the power of Napoleon, it was thus divided into three great portions: the whole of Milan and Venice, with Bologna, the Legations, Romagna, and the Marches, belonged to the kingdom of Italy; Naples, as a separate kingdom, was governed by Murat; Piedmont, as far as the Sesia, Genoa, Parma, Piacenza, Tuscany, and Rome, were merely departments of the French empire. Napoleon, however, sent several members of his family to the government of these French-Italian provinces; giving, for instance, to his sister Eliza, first, the principality of Piombino, then the duchy of Lucca, then the kingdom of Etruria.

In the same manner he entrusted his brother Louis with the Government General of Piedmont, in 1805; and on the elevation of the latter to the throne of Holland, in the following year, the same dignity was conferred upon Napoleon's brother-in-law, Prince Borghese. The French commander of the forces continued, however, to exercise great authority under the nominal auspices of the prince of the blood.

We find nowhere that the people of Piedmont, or of other parts of Italy, expressed at this time any very strong dissatisfaction at the arbitrary *fiat* of a despot, by whom they were bidden to cease to be Italians, and to become French. Nay, from the beginning, annexation to France was, it would seem, proposed by several among the most distinguished Piedmontese, notwithstanding a certain murmur of the multitude. But, after Marengo, the country seemed to have no vote one way or another: we hear, at any rate, of no deputation, either from Turin, Genoa, or Parma, proceeding to Paris, to pray that their lot might be cast together with that of their brethren of the Italian republic or kingdom.

It is most probable, indeed, that their request might have been disregarded; for Napoleon wished Italy to be made subservient to the great destinies of France; and much as he affected to despise her people for cowardice, he dreaded too much at least their insubordination, to fancy that united Italy would long remain under the exercise of his overbearing control. Moreover, he placed the 'natural' confines of France, not on the crest of the Alps, but at their foot, much as the German 'patriots' of the present day consider the Mincio or the Adige their 'natural' frontier; and Piedmont must therefore be French, whilst the annexation of Genoa was determined by the First Consul's anxiety to secure the services of her seamen for his impending maritime struggle with England.

Italian nationality was then, as it ever would be, to be won at the sword's point; but it would still have been consoling to read, if not a manly protest, a petition at least, however humble, of the Italians against those decrees which *aggregated* them, literally, that is, added them, like dumb cattle, to the French herd. It is true the Cisalpine, or Italian State, was no less French than the Italian members of the empire; but it had a name, a banner, a language of its own, and such things have a meaning in men's destinies; and it is no less painfully true that Piedmont, Genoa, and Parma renounced such things without an attempt at resistance, without one word of remonstrance.—*Gallenga's History of Piedmont.*

The following reported conversations of Bonaparte at Milan in 1797, and at Boulogne in 1804, may not be unacceptable:—

"What I have hitherto done," said he to them, "is as nothing. I am only at the beginning of my destined career. Do you suppose that I am triumphing in Italy to secure the greatness of the lawyers of the Directory—the Carnots and the Barrasses? Do you suppose that it is to found a republic? What an idea! A republic of 30,000,000 of souls! With our manners;—our vices! How is it possible? It is a chimera, with which the French people are bewitched, but which will pass away like so many others. They want glory, the gratification of their vanity;—but liberty!—they do not understand anything about it.

"Look at the army! The victories we have gained have already restored the French soldier to his true character. I am everything in his eyes. Let the Directory attempt to take away the command from me, and it will soon see who is master. The nation wants a chief who is illustrious by glory, and not by studies, phrases, speeches of ideologists. Give them baubles,—that is sufficient; they will be amused, and will become tractable; provided, however, that you deceive them skilfully as to the end towards which they are going.

"As to your country, M. de Melzi, there are fewer elements of republicanism there than in France, and even less ceremony is needed with it. We can do with it just what we like; but the proper time has not yet come: We must yield to the fever of the moment; and we are going to have here one or two republics of our own making. Monge will arrange all that for us. In the meantime I have already abolished two from the Italian territories; and although they were very aristocratic republics, yet it was there that the greatest public spirit and the best established opinions prevailed. We should have had a good deal of trouble with them in the sequel.

"Moreover, I am resolved on this,—I will never restore Lombardy or Mantua to Austria. I will give her, instead, Venice, and a portion of the *terra firma* belonging to, that old republic."—*Memoirs de Comte Miot de Melito.*

"What I have hitherto done is nothing," said he one day at the camp of Boulogne, to some of those whom he admitted to his intimacy. "There will never be peace in Europe, except under one chief—an emperor whose officers should be kings; who should distribute kingdoms to his lieutenants. Who should make one king of Italy, another king of Bavaria; this man *landammann* of Switzerland; that, *stadtholder* of Holland. All having offices in the imperial household, with such titles as grand cup-bearer, grand pantler, grand equerry, grand huntsman, &c. It may be said that this plan is only an imitation of that upon which the empire of Germany was founded, and that these ideas are not new; but there is nothing absolutely new. Political institutions only roll along in a circle, and we often return to what has already been done."—*Memoirs de Comte Miot de Melito.*

Most persons who paid any attention to the shoal of pamphlets that appeared in France in the spring of 1859, and more especially those said, and with good reason, to have emanated from the Emperor himself, will remember that there were in those pamphlets allusions to the "great design" of Henry IV., King of France. The circumstances of Europe are not what they were at the end of the seventeenth century, but the French were then the allies of England, and the House of Austria was the object aimed at by the projectors of the great design.

An account of that design, derived from the pages of Sully, may not be unacceptable. There are not wanting among us those who preach the doctrine that France, as the head of the Latin race, has a right to the leadership of Europe, and the roots of this curious doctrine will be found in the suggestive pages of Sully's *Memoirs.*

The great design was intended to found in Europe perpetual peace. War was expensive, devastating, useless. "For," says Sully, (and experience has proved the truth of the reflection), "any attempt which shall tend to bring subjection on Europe, or only to the too considerably augmenting of any one of her principal monarchies at the expense of the others, can never be any other than a chimerical and impossible enterprise; there are none of these monarchies whose destruction will not require a concurrence of causes infinitely superior to all human force. The whole, therefore, of what seems proper and necessary to be done is, to support them all in a kind of equilibrium; and whatever prince thinks, and in consequence acts, otherwise, may indeed cause torrents of blood to flow through all Europe, but he will never be able to change her form."

France especially did not desire to augment her territories, Henry, we are asked to believe, was convinced:

> "that the greatest and most solid advantage he could acquire by his conquests, if he distributed them with equity, was a right of being regarded as the sole benefactor and arbitrator of Europe."

> "The basis of the tranquillity of our own, in particular, depends upon preserving it within its present limits. A climate, laws, manners, and language, different from our own; seas, and chains of mountains almost inaccessible, are all so many barriers which we may consider as fixed even by nature. Besides, what is it that France wants? Will she not always be the richest and most powerful kingdom in Europe? It must be granted. All, therefore, which the French have to wish or desire is, that Heaven may grant them pious, good, and wise kings; and that these kings may employ their power in preserving the peace of Europe; for no other enterprise can, truly, be to them either profitable or successful.

> "And this explains to us the nature of the design which Henry IV. was on the point of putting in execution when it pleased God to take him to himself, too soon by some years for the happiness of the world. From hence likewise we may perceive the motives for his pursuing a conduct so opposite to anything that had hitherto been undertaken by crowned heads; and here we may behold what it was that acquired him the title of 'great' His designs were not inspired by a mean and despicable ambition, nor guided by base and partial interests: to render France happy for ever was his desire; and as she cannot perfectly enjoy this felicity unless all Europe likewise partakes of it, so it was

the happiness of Europe in general which he laboured to procure, and this in a manner so solid and durable that nothing should afterwards be able to shake its foundations.

"What reasons could any of the princes of Europe," he asks, "have to oppose it?" and adds:—"What reason, then, could any of them have to oppose it? And if they did not oppose it, how could the house of Austria support itself against powers in whom the desire and pleasure of depriving it of that strength which it had used only to oppress them would have raised against it as many open as it has secret enemies—that is, the whole of Europe? Nor would these princes have any reason to be jealous of the restorer of their liberty; for he was so far from seeking to reimburse himself for all the expenses which his generosity would hereby engage him in, that his intention was to relinquish voluntarily and forever all power of augmenting his dominions; not only by conquest, but by every other just and lawful means.

"By this he would have discovered the secret of convincing all his neighbours that his whole desire was to save both himself and them those immense sums which the maintenance of so many thousand soldiers, so many fortified places, and so many military expenses require; to free them forever from the fear of those bloody catastrophes so common in Europe; to procure them an uninterrupted repose; and, finally, to unite them all in an indissoluble bond of security and friendship, after which they might live together like brethren, and reciprocally visit like good neighbours, without the trouble of ceremony, and without the expense of a train of attendants, which princes use at best only for ostentation, and frequently to conceal their misery."

The design went upon a religious basis. In all countries the dominant religion was to remain dominant. All existing sects of Christians were to be strengthened, but new sects were to be carefully suppressed on their first appearance. In Italy, Spain, and elsewhere, those who did not like to submit to the rules laid down by the dominant religion were to quit the country or conform.

Another point of the political scheme, which also concerns religion, relates to the infidel princes of Europe, and consists in forcing those entirely out of it who refuse to conform to any of the Christian doctrines of religion. Should the Grand Duke of Muscovy, or Czar of Russia, who is believed to be the ancient Khan of Scythia, refuse to enter into the association after it is proposed to him, he ought to be treated like the Sultan of Turkey, deprived of his possessions in Europe, and confined to Asia only, where he might, as long as he pleased, without any interruption from us, continue the wars in which he is almost constantly engaged against the Turks and Persians.

After describing the strength of the quotas to be furnished by the several States to form what we may term the Federal army, Sully says:—

That part of the design which may be considered as purely political, turned almost entirely on a first preliminary, which, I think, would not have met with more difficulty than the preceding article. This was to divest the house of Austria of the empire, and of all the possessions in Germany, Italy, and the Low Countries; in a word, to reduce it to the sole kingdom of Spain, bounded by the Ocean, the Mediterranean, and the Pyrenean mountains. But that it might, nevertheless, be equally powerful with the other sovereignties of Europe, it should have Sardinia, Majorca, Minorca, and the other islands on its own coasts; the Canaries, the Azores, and Cape Verd, with its possessions in Africa; Mexico, and the American islands which belong to it, countries which alone might suffice to found great kingdoms; finally, the Philippines, Goa, the Moluccas, and its other possessions in Asia.

From hence a method seems to present itself, by which the house of Austria might be indemnified for what it would be deprived of in Europe, which is to increase its dominions in the three other parts of the world, by assisting it to obtain, and by declaring it the sole proprietor, both of what we do know, and what we may hereafter discover in those parts.

And, further on, he continues:—

As to the possessions of the house of Austria in Germany, Italy, and the Low Countries, of which it was to be deprived, not to mention here how much it is indebted for them to a tyrannical usurpation, it would, after all, be only depriving it of territories which it keeps at so prodigious an expense (I speak in particular of Italy and the Low Countries), as all its treasures of the Indies have not been able to defray; and besides, by investing it with the exclusive privilege above mentioned, of gaining new establishments, and appropriating to its own use the mines and treasures of the three other parts of the world, it would be abundantly indemnified; for these new acquisitions would be at least as considerable, and undoubtedly far more rich, than those.

But what is here proposed must not be understood as if the other nations of Europe were excluded from all commerce to those countries; on the contrary, it should be free and open to everyone; and the house of Austria, instead of considering this stipulation, which is of the greatest consequence, as an infringement of its privileges, would rather have reason to regard it as a further advantage.

From a further examination and consideration of these dispositions, I do not doubt but the house of Austria would have accepted the proposed conditions without being forced to it. But, supposing the contrary, what would a resistance have signified? The promise made to all the princes of Europe, of enriching themselves by the territories of which this house was to be divested, would deprive it of all hopes of assistance from any of them.

The Empire of Germany was again to be open to all German princes, and the first emperor was to be the Elector of Bavaria.

The rest of these territories were to have been divided and equally distributed by the Kings of France, England, Denmark, and Sweden, among the Venetians, the Grisons, the Duke of Wurtemberg, and the Marquis of Baden, Anspach, and Dourlach. Bohemia was to have been constituted an elective kingdom, by annexing it to Moravia, Silesia, and Lusatia. Hungary was also to have been an elective kingdom, and the Pope, the Emperor, the Kings of France, England, Denmark, Sweden, and Lombardy, were to have had the right of nomination to it; and because this kingdom may be considered as the barrier of Christendom against the infidels, it was to have been rendered the most powerful and able to resist them; and this was to have been done by immediately adding to it the Archduchy of Austria, Styria, Carinthia, and Carniola, and by afterwards incorporating with it whatever might be acquired in Transylvania, Bosnia, Sclavonia, and Croatia.
The same electors were to have obliged themselves, by oath, to assist it upon all occasions; and they were to have been particularly careful never to grant their suffrages from partiality, artifice, or intrigue, but always to confer the dignity on a prince who, by his great qualifications, particularly for war, should be generally acknowledged as most proper. Poland being, from its nearness to Turkey, Muscovy, and Tartary, in the same situation with Hungary, was also to have been an elective kingdom, by the same eight potentates, and its power was to have been augmented, by annexing to it whatever should be conquered from the infidels adjoining to its own frontiers, and by determining in its favour those disputes which it had with all its other neighbours.

Switzerland, when augmented by Franche-Comté, Alsace, the Tyrol, and other territories, was to have been united into a sovereign republic, governed by a council or senate, of which the emperor, the princes of Germany, and the Venetians were to have been umpires.

The changes to be made in Italy were, that the pope should be declared a secular prince, and bear rank among the monarchs of Europe, and under this title should possess Naples, Apulia, Calabria, and all their dependencies, which should be indissolubly united to St. Peter's patrimony; but in case the holy father had opposed this—which, indeed, could scarcely have been supposed—the disposition must then have been changed, and the kingdom of Naples would have been divided and disposed of as the electoral kings should have determined.

Sicily was to have been ceded to the republic of Venice, by letters from the same eight principal potentates, upon condition that it should render homage for it to every pope who should bear the title of Immediate Chief of the whole Italian Republic, otherwise, for this reason, called the Republic of the Church. The other members of this republic were to have been Genoa, Florence, Mantua, Modena, Parma, and Lucca, without any alterations in their Government; Bologna and Ferrara were to have been made free cities; and all these governments were every twenty years to have rendered homage to the pope their chief, by the gift of a crucifix of the value of ten thousand crowns.

Of the three great republics of Europe it appears, upon the first glance, that this would have been the most brilliant and the richest Nevertheless, it would not have been so; for what belonged to the Duke of Savoy was not comprised herein. His territories were to have been constituted one of the great monarchies of Europe, hereditary to males and females, and to have borne the title of the kingdom of Lombardy, wherein, beside the territory so called, the Milanese and Montferrat would also have been comprised; and the Duke of Mantua, in exchange for these, was to have the Duchy of Cremona. An authentic testimony of the institution would have been given by the pope, the emperor, and the other sovereigns of the Christian republic.

Then Sully glorifies the moderation of France:

Among all these dismemberings, France, we may observe, received nothing for herself but the glory of distributing them with equity.

And so with England:

In regard to England it was precisely the same. This was a determined point between Elizabeth and Henry—the two princes who were authors of the scheme, probably from an observation made by this Queen—that the Britannic Isles, in all the different states through which they had passed, whether under one or several monarchs, elective or hereditary, as well in the male as female line, and in all the variations of their laws and policy, had never experienced any great disappointments or misfortunes but when their Sovereigns had meddled in affairs out of their little continent. It seems, indeed, as if they were concentred in it even by nature, and their happiness appears to depend entirely on themselves, without having any concerns with their neighbours, provided that they seek only to maintain peace in the three nations subject to them, by governing each according to its own laws and customs.

Some other details of the design are set forth.

"And now, perhaps," continues Sully, "the purport of the design may be perceived, which was to divide Europe equally among a certain number of powers in such a manner, that none of them might have cause either of envy or fear from the possessions or power of the others. The number of them was reduced to fifteen, and they were of three kinds:—six great hereditary monarchies, five elective monarchies, and four sovereign republics. The six hereditary monarchies were France, Spain, England or Britain, Denmark, Sweden, and Lombardy; the five elective monarchies were the Empire, the Papacy or Pontificate, Poland, Hungary, and Bohemia; the four republics were the Venetian, the Italian—or what from its dukes may be called the Ducal—the Swiss, Helvetic or Confederate, and the Belgic or Provincial Republic." The business of regulating this new map was to have been delegated to a "General Council of Europe," modelled on "that of the ancient Amphyctions of Greece."

Here is an anticipation of the views of a certain party in our day:—

It consisted of a certain number of commissioners, ministers, or plenipotentiaries from all the governments of the Christian republic, who were to be constantly assembled as a senate, to deliberate on any affairs which might occur, to discuss the different interests, pacify the quarrels, clear up and determine all the civil, political, and religious affairs of Europe, whether within itself or with its neighbours. The form and manner of proceeding in the senate would have been more particularly determined by the suffrages of the senate itself.

Henry was of opinion that it should be composed of four commissioners from each of the following potentates: the Emperor, the Pope, the Kings of France, Spain, England, Denmark, Sweden, Lombardy, Poland, and the Republic of Venice; and of two only from the other republics and inferior powers, which altogether would have composed a senate of about sixty-six persons, who should have been rechosen every three years.

Henry kept his plans secret, but instructed his agents to make general approaches to them, offers of marriage, and so on, taking great precautions to conceal the map-making scheme.

But no precaution appeared so necessary, nor was more strongly recommended to our negotiators, than to convince all the princes of Europe of the disinterestedness with which Henry was resolved to act on this occasion. This point was indefatigably laboured, and they were convinced of it, when, on the supposition that it would be necessary to have recourse to arms, we strongly protested that the forces, the treasures, and even the person of Henry might be depended on; and this in a manner so generous on his side, that, instead of expecting to be rewarded, or even indemnified for them, he was voluntarily inclined to give the most positive assurances not to reserve to himself a single town, nor the smallest district

We need pursue the matter no farther; sufficient has been quoted to show the extent of this vast design; but one mode of operation, not without parallel in our own time, deserves citation as a curiosity. Henry, having fixed on a moment for anticipating the Emperor in the territories of Cleves and Juliers, was then to publish manifestoes, opening the eyes of all to their true interests.

These manifestoes were composed with the greatest care; a spirit of justice, honesty, and good faith, of disinterestedness and good policy, were everywhere apparent in them; and, without wholly discovering the several changes intended to be made in Europe, it was intimated that their common interest had thus compelled its princes to arm themselves, and not only to prevent the house of Austria from getting possession of Cleves, but also to divest her of the United Provinces, and of whatever else she unjustly possessed; that their intentions were to distribute these territories among such princes and states as were the weakest; that the design was such as could not surely give occasion to a war in Europe: that, though armed, the kings of France and the North rather chose to be mediators in the causes of complaint which Europe, through them, made against the house of Austria, and only sought to determine amicably all differences subsisting among the several princes; and that, whatever was done on this occasion, should be not only with the unanimous consent of all these powers, but even of all their people, who were hereby invited to give in their opinions to the confederate princes: such also would have been the substance of the circular letters which Henry and the associated princes would at the same time have sent to all places subject to them; that so, the people being informed, and joining their suffrages, a universal cry from all parts of Christendom would have been raised against the house of Austria."

The great design was never executed, for the knife of Ravaillac terminated the days of the designer. The Abbé de St. Pierre calls it "the most useful discovery for the benefit of mankind that has yet appeared in the world," and adds that its execution "may, perhaps, be reserved by Providence for the greatest and most capable" of Henry's successors. No doubt it was the Amphyctionic council that charmed the imagination of the peace-loving Abbé. In the inscrutable politics of our day, we do not find traces of a revival of Henry's or Sully's idea; but the "map of 1860," which issued mysteriously from the Paris workshop contemporaneously with the famous pamphlets imputed to the Emperor, was based like Henry's "design" upon the elimination of the Austrian Empire from the European system, and the consolidation of smaller into greater states.

LEONAUR

ALSO FROM LEONAUR

WELLINGTON AND THE PYRENEES CAMPAIGN VOLUME I: FROM VI-TORIA TO THE BIDASSOA *by F. C. Beatson*—The final phase of the campaign in the Iberian Peninsula.

WELLINGTON AND THE INVASION OF FRANCE VOLUME II: THE BIDAS-SOA TO THE BATTLE OF THE NIVELLE *by F. C. Beatson*—The second of Beatson's series on the fall of Revolutionary France published by Leonaur, the reader is once again taken into the centre of Wellington's strategic and tactical genius.

WELLINGTON AND THE FALL OF FRANCE VOLUME III: THE GAVES AND THE BATTLE OF ORTHEZ *by F. C. Beatson*—This final chapter of F. C. Beatson's brilliant trilogy shows the 'captain of the age' at his most inspired and makes all three books essential additions to any Peninsular War library.

NAVAL BATTLES OF THE NAPOLEONIC WARS *by W. H. Fitchett*—Cape St. Vincent, the Nile, Cadiz, Copenhagen, Trafalgar & Others

SERGEANT GUILLEMARD: THE MAN WHO SHOT NELSON? *by Robert Guillemard*—A Soldier of the Infantry of the French Army of Napoleon on Campaign Throughout Europe

WITH THE GUARDS ACROSS THE PYRENEES by *Robert Batty*—The Experiences of a British Officer of Wellington's Army During the Battles for the Fall of Napoleonic France, 1813.

A STAFF OFFICER IN THE PENINSULA *by E. W. Buckham*—An Officer of the British Staff Corps Cavalry During the Peninsula Campaign of the Napoleonic Wars

THE LEIPZIG CAMPAIGN: 1813—NAPOLEON AND THE "BATTLE OF THE NATIONS" *by F. N. Maude*—Colonel Maude's analysis of Napoleon's campaign of 1813.

BUGEAUD: A PACK WITH A BATON by *Thomas Robert Bugeaud*—The Early Campaigns of a Soldier of Napoleon's Army Who Would Become a Marshal of France.

TWO LEONAUR ORIGINALS

SERGEANT NICOL by *Daniel Nicol*—The Experiences of a Gordon Highlander During the Napoleonic Wars in Egypt, the Peninsula and France.

WATERLOO RECOLLECTIONS by *Frederick Llewellyn*—Rare First Hand Accounts, Letters, Reports and Retellings from the Campaign of 1815.

www.ingramcontent.com/pod-product-compliance
Lightning Source LLC
Chambersburg PA
CBHW021058090426
42738CB00006B/405